EVERY LEAST SPARROW

4-19-17

Dear Joan —

_ Every _Least_ _Sparrow_ — what a
heart wrenching account of
a mother's love for her impaired
child! Her strength a courage is
unbelievable. Her articulation
in writing this is so well done.
Thanks for Sharing. In my notes
on Anne Lamont's 'Small Victories

they were Not unfavorable —
(experiences in her life + ours)

Betty Jay
age 91

EVERY LEAST SPARROW

CAROLYN H. WALKER

GARN PRESS
NEW YORK, NY

Published by Garn Press, LLC
New York, NY
www.garnpress.com

Excerpts from this book have appeared in various literary journals – "Lovebird" in *Hunger Mountain: The Vermont College Journal of Arts & Letters*; "Sanctuary" in *The Southern Review*; and "Bird Effect" under the title "From Circling Jennifer: A Mother and Daughter Odyssey" in *Columbia: A Journal of Literature and Art*.

Book and cover design by Benjamin J. Taylor/Garn Press
Cover image by Rena Brouwer

First Edition, January 2017

Library of Congress Control Number: 2016954493

Publisher's Cataloging-in-Publication Data

Names: Walker, Carolyn H.
Title: Every least sparrow / Carolyn H. Walker.
Description: New York : Garn Press, 2017.
Identifiers: LCCN 2016954493 | ISBN 978-1-942146-50-6 (pbk.) | ISBN 978-1-942146-51-3 (hardcover) | ISBN 978-1-942146-52-0 (Kindle ebook)
Subjects: LCSH: Parents of children with disabilities--Biography. | Children with disabilities--Biography. | Mothers and daughters--Biography. | Syndromes in children--Popular works. | Developmental disabilities. | BISAC: BIOGRAPHY & AUTOBIOGRAPHY / People with Disabilities. | FAMILY & RELATIONSHIPS / Parenting / Motherhood. | FAMILY & RELATIONSHIPS / Children with Special Needs. | EDUCATION / Special Education / Developmental & Intellectual Disabilities. | BIOGRAPHY & AUTOBIOGRAPHY / Personal Memoirs
Classification: LCC HQ759.913 .W35 2016 (print) | LCC HQ759.913 (ebook) | DDC 305.9/085092--dc23.

For Jennifer and Dr. James O'Neill

**So I still don't know what IQ is,
and everybody says it's something different.**

**Charlie Gordon, in *Flowers for Algernon* by
Daniel Keyes**

Contents

Preface - Dr. Raoul Hennekam

There you are. A doctor has just told you your child has a syndrome. A syndrome: even just that word, it sounds already ominous. In fact you know only of Down syndrome. But Rubinstein-Taybi syndrome? Never heard of it. You have all kinds of questions, but then it becomes clear your GP and your pediatrician have never seen a child with this syndrome either, so they can hardly help.

What to expect? Are there medical problems? Should a child with this syndrome be under control for these, and can you prevent anything? How about medications? Can your child go to school later on, or marry, or have children? How is it to have a child with this syndrome? Will you be able to cope with it? Can you go on having a job? Will it influence your relationship with your partner or your other children?

As always the best information can be obtained from those who are dealing with children with the syndrome most: the children themselves and their parents! The present book is written by such a parent, and offers a wealth of information. Surely about the syndrome itself. But, more importantly, how the life is of a family in which a child with Rubinstein-Taybi syndrome is born. The shock, the disbelief, the uncertainties, the anxieties. But also the unexpected joys, the warmth and care of people of whom you hadn't expected it, the laughter, the love.

The book is written in a marvelous style, and is open, in every sense of the word. The book teaches you also how to look into the world through the eyes of someone with the syndrome, and you will read it is usually a beautiful world.

The word syndrome? Please just forget it. Read this marvelous book, cry and laugh, and enjoy.

Raoul Hennekam, MD PhD
Professor of Pediatrics and Translational Genetics, University of Amsterdam
Medical Advisor of Rubinstein-Taybi support groups (several countries)
Amsterdam, June 2016

Author's Note

With the exceptions of Dr. James O'Neill, Dr. Craig Spangler, and Jacqueline Sullivan, who gave permission for their names to be used, the names of other secondary characters have been changed to protect privacy.

For the present generation, the word "retard*ed*" has become as disagreeable as the epithet "retard." I have chosen to use the word "retard*ed*" because that was the accepted medical and educational term used to describe Jennifer when she was growing up.

The title for the book was suggested by the poem, *Easter, Looking Westward*, by Kimberly Johnson.

Introduction

These were our halcyon days. Every day a dream, our lives vessels of anticipation. Love letters flew back and forth like tireless birds. Ticket stubs and trinkets took the form of treasure, especially the two plastic hearts with jig-sawed edges that fit together as seamlessly as man and woman. They were garnet-red and slight as petals, and we each kept one in a pocket, something to hold when we were apart.

Don, 30, had saved them for years waiting for the woman he thought might never arrive.

I was that woman, the 17-year-old optimist who came strolling into his judo class one Saturday. He was the brooding, darkly-handsome mystery that consumed me. After a shameless flirtation, I offered him my hand. He clasped it and, two years later, we strolled through a beautiful autumn afternoon into the campus theater at the university where I was a student. We took seats in the dark. We leaned into one another, the light from the screen illuminating our faces as *Charly* began. We watched while Charlie Gordon (Charly in the movie), a man undergoing experimental treatment for his mental retardation, kept pace with the mouse Algernon, cured of his deficiencies, but of course doomed. Don and I understood, in particular, when Charlie fell in love. We were there, filled with love's intoxicating promises and tingling pleasures. When the movie was over, we exited the theater whispering about Charlie's predicament. Sunshine colored the world that awaited us on the other side of the glass doors.

I Bring Forth A Rarity

I'm embarrassed to say I no longer remember the time of day, or even the day of the week it was when Jennifer was born. It seems to me it was late in the afternoon, but my sense of time surrounding her birth has less to do with the hour than with the colors that accompanied her arrival. These I remember – the dulled creams, the ambers and crimsons and browns that evoked the slow but inevitable passing of a day into night.

I remember, in fact I can still feel, how the colors blanketed the activities in the delivery room, how they warmed and nurtured me as the saddle block anesthesia drained from my spine, freeing my legs so that I could roll onto my belly in the recovery bed. I made myself comfortable after six hours of hard pushing, entering into a sweet postpartum repose.

During the last three months of this pregnancy, Jennifer had taxed my capacity to expand. Though she would weigh in at a mere five pounds and six ounces, a tiny seventeen inches long, she and the amniotic waters that cradled her had stretched my belly far beyond the limits to which my son Matthew and daughter Holly had taken it.

With Jennifer, I became an undulating summer landscape, my stomach its central mountain, my swollen nose and cheeks and knees and ankles the nearby hills.

Overdue to give birth in the heat of late July, I counted the passing days and became increasingly expectant. I wanted this baby out where I could enjoy her. I therefore appreciated my obstetrician when he finally probed deep inside me, deliberately rupturing the membranes that kept her safe, hidden.

Later, as I settled into my room alone, I gave an audible sigh, a contented *ah* as comfort and satisfaction claimed me. Like me, Don was not aware that something was amiss, and, tired from the long day, but full of joy, he had gone home to help his mother tend to Holly, whom he would bring to visit on day three.

The soft mattress welcomed my engorged breasts, my exhausted belly, my legs and toes, my face. Lying there, waiting to hold my baby for the first time, I closed my eyes and drifted in and out of my own awe – *I have another daughter.* I played with possible names for her, cognizant of the way names carry connotations for a lifetime. Prudence. Ginger. Rose. Faith. Belle. Fanny. Candy.

Carolyn. I heard my name come tentatively through the curtains that separated my cubicle from those of two other women. I ignored it the first time, certain that the call must be meant for someone else. The name came again, raced off a man's tongue, insistent. *Carolyn. Carolyn.* I turned to see our pediatrician parting the curtains and pushing his way toward me.

Even in the semi-darkness I could see that Dr. O'Neill's eyes were working to take me in – searching to determine how I felt, how I was thinking, what I was thinking. The space between us was charged, as if we were two electrical forces exchanging a current of expectation. I leaned toward him, curiosity riding on my face, but Dr. O'Neill spoke before I could form even the simplest *How's my baby?* He steadied his body, braced it, and summoned his resolve.

"I've been in the library researching for hours," he started, and I was caught off guard, briefly mystified. I had no idea what a library had, at that very moment, to do with me.

"I think your baby has a syndrome." Dr. O'Neill paused, allowing his words to reach me. They sparked and snapped, and I felt my heart lurch against them. My shoulders seized and the new-mother happiness drained from my face.

"What do you mean?" I was upright now.

Dr. O'Neill began to spout gibberish – "Spatula thumbs … webbed neck … cathedral palate … beak nose …"

I recoiled, blinked, gaped. From out of an inescapable fear that already perceived the truth, I conjured the question I most dreaded to ask, not really understanding why I felt compelled to ask it, only knowing that I must. The question was reflexive, primal, under pressure. It surfaced like a wad of hot gastric juice, and I spat it at Dr. O'Neill – "Will she be retarded?" I didn't think to ask if the baby might die. I instinctively knew she wouldn't. Although I had not yet seen her up close, I knew just as surely as Dr. O'Neill stood before me that I had given birth to a child who would live, but never lead a normal life.

Dr. O'Neill attempted to both inform and comfort me with his answer. He chose his words quickly, but carefully, veiling them in a modified truth that was meant to shore up hope and protect us both.

"No, she'll be slow to walk, slow to talk, but she'll learn to read." He emphasized these skills, their possibilities, as if they contained the key to human happiness. His voice drifted off and he came to give me a hug, the kind he reserved for congratulating new mothers. As he did so, I felt the cage of irrevocable, unalterable change close around me.

Dr. O'Neill's hug betrayed his uncertainty, but because I felt sorry that he had been made this unfortunate messenger, I met his compassion with a measure of my own. I hugged him back, and I let him escape with his lie.

The night passed, close and oppressive like a stalker, but no one dared to remove the baby from the intensive care nursery where she was being monitored and bring her to me.

In the same way, no one came to escort me down the hall to her. I had all the urges and longings of a healthy mother, but I had a complicated birthing history and no personal reference point from which to measure a normal experience. Our first child Matthew, who was delivered prematurely, had died from under-developed lungs when he was one day old. Holly, also premature, had been hustled to the specialized preemie nursery as a precaution before I could so much as get a good look at her. Not knowing what else to do, I waited this morning for someone with authority to take action.

Just after dawn, a nurse came to awaken me. Poised with my breakfast and a blood pressure cuff, she shoved aside the curtain and found me, a quivering mass, sitting up in bed. "What's the matter?" she asked, although she most surely knew.

"I want to see my baby," I said. "I haven't seen my baby. Dr. O'Neill said there's something wrong with her."

Neither my heart nor my mind could envision what I had given birth to. Was my baby a modern day incarnation of the Brenda of my childhood – a composite of overlaid circles? I remembered how Brenda, a gargantuan among splashing toddlers, gently placed her inflated black inner tube onto the waves of Sylvan Lake, and how she mounted that inner tube and cork bobbed, a fat round adult with a fat round head that housed a fat round face with wide round eyes and an expressionless O mouth.

Was she another Linda Lou, her form a series of contorted, junior high angles? I shuddered, ashamed at the way I once shrank down into my skin, made myself invisible, and let those two eighth-grade boys goad the clueless Linda Lou – "Hey, wanna go on a date?"

All that I assumed to be true about mental retardation I had gleaned while observing these two young women as they passed through my adolescence and into my nightmares – Nature's cruelest joke.

"I'll go get her," the nurse said, surprising me. She turned and left and, my heart quickening, I called after her, wondering if it was safe, but my words fell short. Within moments she returned with a pink baby, squirming in an equally pink blanket in her arms. She handed the baby to me and said, "Go ahead, peel back the blanket and count her fingers and toes." The nurse smiled, knowing I needed to run my hands over the chest, feel the heart beat beneath it, bend the arms and legs, caress the forehead with my lips.

The nurse knew I would fall in love with this baby, that all it would take to make things right would be for me to hold her in my arms. She handed her to me, then sat on the edge of my bed and watched while I tentatively turned the blanket back from the baby's head. Its hemmed corner unfolded like the flap of an envelope, revealing first a spray of thick dark hair, and then a narrow face, crinkled as if to cry. Surprised by the light and perhaps the sound of my familiar heartbeat, the baby abandoned her cry, blinked her eyes, and attempted to study me.

I noticed that a large red birthmark patched her forehead, a stark contrast in color to those eyes. The soft spot at her crown yawned down into a cleft beneath the birthmark, almost touching her eyebrows. Its skin pulsed in rhythm with her heartbeat, as if a gentle drummer drummed beneath it. She raised her eyebrows then squinted. She puckered her lips, wanting to suck. She pushed her tongue out, groping for a nipple.

"Look at all that hair," I said to the nurse, delight emerging in my voice. I didn't know the baby's hair shouldn't creep so far across the hairline. I brushed my thumb under it, across the birthmark, and began imagining baby hairdos with pink bows.

"The birthmark will fade with time," the nurse offered.

Then came, "Look at that nose!" I marveled, as it seemed so self-assured. It was an honest to goodness nose, a nose that was confident in its task.

The nurse urged me to proceed, to check everything, to reassure myself that here in this tenuous package lived a whole human being. And so I explored my daughter, observing and touching cautiously. I slid the blanket fully away, exposing her torso and tiny diaper then delicately pinched her thumbs, first one and then the other, between the tips of my forefinger and thumb.

They were a mystery to me. Jointless in their centers, they resisted bending, except at the base. When I released them, the baby tucked them to her palms and folded her fingers over them, instinctively protecting them. Her fists seemed only a little larger than a pair of marbles.

I moved my gaze to the big toes. The left one, thick and rounded, looked like a Lilliputian baseball bat. The right was doubled, shaped like a heart, and contained two square toenails, side-by-side windows overlooking a simple view of fresh baby flesh.

I turned her over in my hands and ran my fingers the length of her back, feeling a fine layer of invisible, downy hair. She was as warm and fuzzy as an African violet that had spent an afternoon in the sun. She drooped her head with trust over my palm. She allowed this touching, the way a drowsy lap cat allows petting. I stroked her and found another birthmark at the nape of her neck, and then down, a deep, furry dot at the base of her spine.

"The doctor says she has a syndrome," I said. My voice was a whisper. My eyes met the nurse's. She gestured at the dot, and meant well when she called it a "little tail".

"That's one of the syndrome traits," the nurse said.

"I don't want a child with a tail. I don't understand what all this means," I said.

The nurse stood and scurried from my room a second time, returning promptly with a large, navy blue medical book, nearly the size of a dictionary. "There's information in here about the syndrome." She urged the book towards me. Across its cover, in big block letters of tarnished gold, the book read, "MENTAL RETARDATION SYNDROMES."

I grew flushed, more confused, but the nurse didn't notice as she opened the book and skimmed the table of contents, then thumbed through the pages. I began to rock, a helpless child myself, but the nurse didn't notice as she displayed an old, black-and-white photograph of a nameless adolescent girl.

The girl, who had Rubinstein-Taybi Syndrome, had a careless pageboy haircut with greasy bangs that were too short. She had a caricature face, and like the unfortunate Quasimodo was contorted, twisted, misaligned. Her thick eyebrows attempted to merge on her forehead, her nose reached off the page, her grin clawed its way up to her cheekbones, her teeth protruded and crossed each other, her chin receded into her neck, and her eyes, set in down-sloped sockets, refused to release mine.

Don made his first visit alone, just after the nurse's presentation, arriving expectantly and with a blissful jaunt in his step. As he skipped into my hospital room, I greeted him with my newly long face and tried to paraphrase Dr. O'Neill's words in a forceful blast, which up until that moment had been every bit as under pressure as water simmering in a closed hydrant on a blistering summer's day.

"Dr. O'Neill thinks the baby has a syndrome." The word *syndrome* came out of me surrounded by tears and a jettison of spit, like this – *S-S-SIN-drome,* as if I were some backwoods, snake-handling preacher spewing hell and damnation. Don stopped listening when he heard the word. His body went still, and his gaze, betraying alarm, looked to the floor.

Many long minutes passed. They hung in the air between us like icicles. I finally broke the silence with a tirade of her symptoms, gleaned from the haze of post-delivery, but they made no more sense to him than they did to me. I watched while Don winced against cathedral palate and spatula thumbs and beak nose. Then I bespoke the trickle down fear that had welled up inside me during the night. "Do you think you'll be able to love her?"

I pressed the weight of this question into my eyes. Felt the swell of my face around them. I understood the way my eyes and face swung on the front of me, the way they were laden with anticipation and the importance of what would be his response. I needed him to love this inscrutable baby and I needed him to do it now. I contemplated the marital rift that I feared would accompany the word *no*.

Don shrugged his shoulders, stuffed his hands into his pockets and pivoted away. "We'll see," he said, I think not so much doubting his capacity to love as gathering himself from what must have felt like a lashing.

Don looked like Rodin's *The Thinker* on day three, sitting there next to my bed in the metal and pea-green plastic chair, his fist propping up his chin, his elbow on his knee. His hair was combed neatly away from his face in the same style he had worn since high school. His cotton shirt clung to his form, the sleeves rolled, like always, up his forearms. We were slinging names around the room, wishing that one would boomerang back to us, a perfect fit for our baby.

"How about Stephanie," he said, peering at me, but I didn't like the name any more. I had liked it once, but now it didn't seem right. It was too long, longer than our new daughter's body. I suggested Tina, knowing that it wouldn't fit either. Its spelling implied the unfortunate and obvious *tiny*. Don swung his head *no.*

I then suggested Jennifer for its beauty. Oh I know, it's only one letter shorter than Stephanie, but it doesn't have all those loops and hurdles, doesn't flail around on the tongue quite so much. "We could call her Jenny, or Jen," I suggested, urging. I harbored affection for the romance that surrounded the name, the way it's derived from Guinevere.

Don and I batted the name back and forth sounding out its variations, finding ourselves in agreement, and then we pondered some companion names to go in the middle, between Jennifer and Walker. We struck a bargain with Jennifer Laurie. Jennifer after my Guinevere fancy, and Laurie in honor of my sister, Jennifer Laurie Walker Rubinstein Taybi, born July 30, 1977.

That evening we introduced Holly – she swinging her way on Don's arm up the hospital corridor, throwing herself and a gift of M & Ms into my embrace, then stopping with an abrupt awareness of her surroundings, her eyes rounded and her belly pooched forward, toddler style.

She turned quietly and toed her way up the floorboards to make herself taller, her auburn hair sweeping her shoulders, an index finger slinking its way up to her nose, where it rubbed an itch as she considered the newborns. Studious even at age four, she peered through the nursery window without speaking before looking to Don and me for confirmation. We stooped in, flanked her cheeks with our own, singled Jennifer out from the others. Speaking one of us into each of her ears, we held Holly in the stereo of our whispers, soft but nevertheless energized. "There's your sister."

In the presenting of our daughters, Don and I felt happiness, at once assertive and inevitable, sidle its way into our little throng. Holly pressed her lips to the glass as if she were going to make a blow fish face by way of welcoming Jennifer into the world. Beyond it, Jennifer wriggled like a beetle on its back, the glow of the nursery lights blanketing us all.

The following morning, just before he discharged Jennifer and me by proxy, Dr. O'Neill faced down some more of my questions. One of them was a nagging question born of my emerging denial, which would swell and last for Jennifer's first five years, until she was old enough for kindergarten and I could do no more pretending.

"Is there a chance she could be normal?" I clung to that word *normal* like it was a lifeline. A mother's dreams can shape-shift with surprising speed. In less than a week, mine had shrunk, flip-flopped, all but disappeared. I no longer cared that Jennifer might not run for the United States presidency, or place in an Olympic decathlon, or be an honor student. Everyday normal would be good enough for me.

Dr. O'Neill nodded his head in a slow acquiescence. He allowed that it was possible she might grow to be a normal girl with no more strikes against her than those strange thumbs and even stranger toes. Granting me permission to take Jennifer home, he tried to make the leaving easy. "Take her home and love her," he said – six simple syllables to inform the duration of our lives. In an earlier generation, he would one day admit, he might have suggested that Jennifer be institutionalized.

We Begin

Because Don rarely talks about his pre-Carolyn life, I have to guess at the reasons why. In so doing, I call upon two stereotypes. He is of German heritage – fifty-percent on his mother's side – and he grew up in an impoverished alcoholic home. I never knew his father, who died before we met, but Don has leaked enough information for me to surmise that his family lived in the kind of heartache so often associated with alcoholism – unpredictability, unmet needs, suppressed emotions, tensions, shame, and secrecy. Though he's never said as much, I assume Don learned to fade into the background as a means of self-preservation, a behavior so ingrained and unexamined that he has carried it into adulthood, spending marriage and fatherhood in the shadows.

Don told me once, in an unusual moment of candor, that one day he came home from school to find his father passed out on the sidewalk, and that he was not strong enough to move him. When he tried, his father's head bounced off the pavement and he was forced to leave him there. I pictured this – an old man's balding head going up and down on the cement like a basketball, Don's face twisted in effort, his scrawny arms straining against the impossible, the two of them creating an unfortunate display for the neighbors.

This story evokes compassion in me not only for the boy Don was forced to be, but for the boy he might have been under different circumstances. Old report cards reveal his potential in excellent grades, and trophies his talent for basketball and golf. Cherished greeting cards and notes portray a romantic. School photographs show the counterpoint – a lonely, straight-faced child, year after year, with sad, longing eyes. Not one of them so much as hints at a smile.

My experience in childhood could not have been more different. I sometimes came home from school to find my mother practicing yoga headstands in the center of the living room. Her toes would be pointed toward the ceiling, her rump tucked in, her fingers wound into the crown of her auburn hair, her forearms spread on the carpeting so that her elbows fashioned a triangle with her head. As I passed into the foyer she would fold herself down onto the floor and welcome me with conversation.

I delighted in my mother and grew up wanting to be like her. She loved life, and fun, and people, and varied experience. She and my father, a reserved, faithful man, treated my sister, Laurie, and me to an idyllic childhood filled with opportunity – family trips, pets, theater, church, music lessons, beach time, and plenty of laughter.

It was this kind of life I wanted to share with Don, and I had no reason to imagine it would be elusive. We were happy and optimistic in our love, and in it I hoped to make up for all he'd missed. Of course I know now, as a sixty-four-year-old woman, that that was the fantasy of a teenage girl. I don't wish to malign my imagination, however. Over the years, it has been a blessing to me, treating me to lofty dreams and notions, even as it oppressed me with horrors when I let it fly.

I first met Don when I was a junior in high school in 1967, and I'd spent months thinking about him, romanticizing him, wallowing in infatuation and my sexual awakening, plotting ways to put myself in his path. Dark haired, dark eyed, well built, mysterious, and thirteen years older than me, he was virile and handsome. He seemed grounded, not gad-about and fickle like the boys I met at school and work.

I joined his Saturday morning Judo class. I prowled the halls in my bathing suit and its tiny woven cover-up, and conspicuously trotted into the cafeteria where he drank coffee during his free time. I sat with him whenever I could, offering innuendos, cracking jokes, and swooning from across the table when he responded. When he made a casual remark about playing golf, his favorite sport, I manipulated him into a commitment to teach me, although he seemed happy enough to do so when the time came.

I first saw Don's house on a summer's night in 1967 when I drove by on my way home from, where? I had been lifeguarding on the evening shift at the YMCA, perhaps. Or maybe I'd been to town to see my best friend, Joy. Don taught Judo part-time at the Y, and we had not been able to meet that night as we increasingly did during our spare time. So I swung by his home, having looked up the address in the phone book and the nearest cross streets on a map.

When I made my first left turn onto East Sheffield Street, I braked and shifted and cranked the steering wheel of my old Chevy around, my gaze penetrating the dark in search of the number 29. I wouldn't stop to talk to Don. I just wanted to see how he lived, what his house looked like. I didn't think of myself as an obsessed young woman. Nor did I think of myself as a spy, although that was most surely what I was.

Don's house, silhouetted by the streetlights, matched most of those in his neighborhood. They were single-family, starter homes with chain link fences, one-car driveways and sidewalks that led to two-step stoops. They had windows flanking their front doors, the left exposing bedrooms, the right their living rooms.

I eased the Chevy against the curb opposite his house and put it in neutral, and the car and I sat. I rolled my window down and simply observed, as if I were at a drive-in theater, enthralled by one of the year's movies – *Guess Who's Coming to Dinner?*, *In Like Flint,* or maybe *House of a Thousand Dolls.*

The houses were small, lined up in an uneven row like a child's blocks. The neighborhood, which rolled gently downhill in an easterly direction, was quiet but not yet asleep. Lamplight yellowed the living room windows of each house, and a glow seeped through the curtains of Don's and out into the night air. Just outside the house, just beyond a big shrub, his midnight-blue Grand Prix waited in the driveway. I longed to knock on the door and go inside for a visit, but lacked the nerve to do so. After sitting for a while, I engaged first gear and pulled away.

Driving home, I wondered about Don's widowed mother, Clara. I knew that she lived with him because he had told me. He had purchased the house after his father died, and she had stayed on, preparing meals and keeping house. I imagined her to be a plump and pleasant woman, a cheery, warm soul with hair and eyes the shade of Don's, rouge-colored cheeks, and a welcoming smile.

I wouldn't discover she was a toothless hunchback until Don and I became engaged two years later and I met her for the first time. And it wouldn't be until after we were married and I'd moved into the house on East Sheffield Street that I'd learn she was an armchair clairvoyant, divining people's futures by "reading" a deck of playing cards. I never asked her to read my fortune, but she one day volunteered, long after the fact, that she knew Matthew would die. *What good is a prediction that comes too late?* I thought.

I gave no credence to Clara's predictions until Jennifer

was born and I became desperate for any sign of good news or promise. I clung to her words when she assured me, "Jennifer will be all right," her eyes two puddles filled with the murky unknown.

I also remember the first time Don visited my family home in 1969, its shrub and tree filled acre overlooking a roiling creek. We were new to it, and my father had taken pains to tend the grass and plant his favorite trees and flowers. The setting was pastoral and quiet except for the sounds of the creek and the occasional bird chirp. The sun was shining and Don and I stood side-by-side watching the water move in front of us. "This is every man's dream," he said. He smiled and gave a faint nod, his appreciation flooding me with warmth and desire.

Coming Home

Years after she'd become an adult, Holly would share her recollection of the day Jennifer came into the world – "What I remember is that the stars were out and the sun was trying to come up."

I love this memory not only for its metaphoric optimism, but because of the way it looks now transferred into my mind – a deep blue fading into a cobalt blue, and then the cobalt becoming morning. I picture the stars winking above us as Don and I rush off to the hospital, the sun rising to eclipse them. I see Holly standing at her bedroom window, her long hair draped over her shoulders, her pajamas askew on her little body, watching as our car drives away, her eyes rising from the red of our taillights to search the sky.

Less hope oversaw our trip home from the hospital. All that I remember of it is the way our Pontiac's drone mesmerized Don and me along the way. If the car carried us literally, the drone carried us figuratively, Don's and my thoughts, and any conversation that might have accompanied them, suspended in its two-note, hum-thrum melody. I must have carried Jennifer in my arms, and Don must have held the door when I tossed "We have another girl!" over the fence to our curious neighbor. And I must have kissed Holly hello when we entered the kitchen through the back door out of habit. Don's mother Clara, there to babysit Holly, must have *oohed* and *aahed* when we pressed her new granddaughter into her arms for the first time. And we must all have headed for the living room, where we must have gathered our collective breath and set about establishing the routine that would measure, like a heart with tachycardia, the rest of what would become our increasingly compartmentalized lives.

Don and I were not what I would call unhappy or joyous, when we brought Jennifer home. It was more like we were shell shocked, unsure how to get our bearings. We weren't sure what to think, or do, or expect. We held her and fed her and changed her diaper and cooed and marveled at her little life. But we didn't take on parenting her with the same gusto I remember taking on with Holly. We spent time studying Jennifer, wondering what *this* meant, and what *that* meant. We touched her as if we were afraid she would break, and we kept our guard up.

We had no idea how to tell our friends Jennifer had been born with disabilities, or even if we should draw this to their attention. Family members knew, of course, because they had visited her in the hospital. But our friends had no clue, nor did any of them have handicapped children who might help them identify with our situation.

Telling them would mean that Don and I would have to summon a new vocabulary and rein in our emotions. I wanted our friends' understanding but worried they might pity us instead. At the time, on top of Matthew's death, it was easy to view Jennifer's condition as a cruel twist, too easy to do in our lives built around assumptions, prejudices, a lack of experience, and fear.

When I received our friends' phone calls assuming all

was well, I hmmed and hawed, searching for words that would describe our new truth. "The doctor says Jennifer has a syndrome, but we don't know which one yet." Their knee-jerk silence told me the word *syndrome* was as foreign to them as it was to Don and me. I was filled with gratitude and a deep relief when they came to the house with baby gifts and told me she was beautiful.

It is with this scene that my memories come into better focus – Jennifer, scarcely more than a spot on the mattress of the crib we had prepared for her. This crib of cream-colored wood had welcomed me twenty-seven years prior, and then my sister Laurie, and later Holly, my mother and father having stored it in their basement all those years. Nostalgia and the comfort of family ties were as much a part of this crib as the pink lamb decals that adorned its headboard.

The first time I placed Jennifer in it, though, I felt as if I were handing her over to a giant's swallow, its side rails so many fearsome teeth. And so I pulled her from it and used instead the infant carrier given to me by strangers in the emergency room at St. Joseph Mercy Hospital, where I was a clerk, a job I had taken a year before Jennifer was born. I had admired it one night when I helped admit their sick son, and they had surprised me with it when he outgrew it. I wrapped its foam pad in a baby blanket and placed it on the floor beside Don's and my bed, and I nestled Jennifer there. While Don slept, I peeked through its plastic window whenever I awoke in the night, double-checking to make sure Jennifer was still breathing.

We lived like this for the first few weeks of her life. And like any new baby, she roused during the night for feedings, her cries for sustenance as welcome as the pealing of church bells. When she slept, I slept … as well as any woman sleeps with one eye open.

During her third month, while I was home alone with Jennifer, a sound came from her nursery that I did not recognize.

It was not a baby sound. Rather, it was the sound of something else. Snorting, rooting as if in a frantic search. Even from the kitchen I could hear the snarf of its nose as it rubbed against the crib mattress, the rattle in its throat as it took in a series of sharp, quick breaths. I dropped food I was preparing onto the countertop and ran.

The nursery was in semi-darkness, the shades pulled and the light dowsed so that Jennifer could nap. I had turned this room, which by now she shared with Holly, into a little girl haven that was warm and colorful, adorned the walls with orange and yellow flowered wallpaper and pictures, and topped the dresser with knickknacks and stuffed animals. How could one of them have come to life?

Terrified, I found Jennifer on her belly in the crib, her tiny head turned to one side. Her eyes were closed, her lips pursed into small, delicate Vs. As if she were possessed, the animal's snort went in and out of her nostrils, sucked them down, rhythmically against the sheet. Her head followed. One of Jennifer's arms, her right, lay along the length of her body, pressed there, a fulcrum against which the rest of her rode.

The other arm was wound slightly up behind her back. She couldn't be comfortable, the palm of her hand facing the ceiling like that. The arm twitched and jerked. Jennifer twitched and jerked. With each snort, her face rose a little off the mattress, her arm a little off her back, as if strings connected them to a puppeteer. My response was wholly maternal, instinctive and swift, adrenaline driven. I reached over the railing and grabbed her, shoved my hands beneath her legs and shoulders and snatched her up to the safety of my arms. I turned her towards me, whisper-shouting, my breath flooding her face.

"Jennifer! Jennifer!" She opened her eyes and searched for me, surprised that I would awaken her. She was a rag doll in my arms.

I held her close and circled the nursery, trying to get my

composure. Only seconds passed but they carried the weight of hours. The banging of my heartbeat slowed by degrees, and as it did so I hurried to phone Dr. O'Neill. I pressed Jennifer against my left shoulder, the forefinger of my right hand pecking awkwardly at the dial. When I heard the doctor's voice finally come to the other end of the line, I coughed my suffocating fears into his ear. "There's something wrong with the baby. She was jerking in her bed!"

I slid down onto the golden-green carpeting of our home's only hallway, its walls consuming me, and I listened as he tried not to betray alarm in his voice. He spoke with measured, well-practiced words, in a controlled tone. "She could have had a seizure. Children with these kinds of syndromes often do. Better get an EEG."

I hated the way days had to pass before I could get answers to the questions that grieved me. The confusion was mighty, the wait interminable, the nights infinite. I soon discovered it would always be this way in Jennifer's life. I learned the lesson for the first time this day though, and I felt my nerves go on an alert that would be sequentially intensified for decades.

Our scare was just one of scores the technicians at the hospital had to deal with, however, and so two weeks passed before I could get an appointment for Jennifer to have her electroencephalogram – a test used to detect abnormalities related to electrical activity of the brain. On the given day, on our way to the neurology unit, I slinked past my desk in the ER so that my anxiety would not contaminate any of the other clerks, nurses, or doctors I knew.

At long last, on the second floor, a compassionate young technician, who suspected that she recognized me from some-where, threaded electrodes into Jennifer's wispy hair. Jennifer had the look of a peach that had been penetrated by colorful pipe cleaners, and once she was wired, I placed her on a cot and watched while the EEG's pen scratched its message, in a ghostly fashion, onto graph paper. The message came forth in hills and valleys, its swells and dips dictated by Jennifer's brainwaves. There was a beauty to this writing, like that of an ancient script, and it was just as foreign to me. I watched it take form, from left to right, fascinated and fearful at the same time.

When the test was finished, the technician ripped the long page efficiently from the machine and the wires just as efficiently from Jennifer's head. A few days later a neurologist called to say that yes, Jennifer had a seizure disorder. And a few days after that another phoned to say that, no, she didn't. Later, still another sided with the first and a debate ensued. And so it went until Jennifer was in her twenties. Yes, no, yes, no, one thing or another.... Until one night in the late 1990s, when I suddenly realized (could I have dreamt it?) that I had slept a whole night through.

Bird Effect

Ours quickly became a strange kind of celebrity, the kind you have when you own a rare coin that has never been circulated. Doctors, like coin collectors, wanted to look and touch, to discuss and deliver value judgments whenever Jennifer was hospitalized, which was often – croup, pneumonia, cystitis and nephritis having their way with her over and over, mercilessly. Word spread among the doctors like gossip and drew them to pediatrics whether they were pediatricians or not – random herds of fresh-faced interns, eager to learn and impress, and droll specialists who longed to be jarred from the routine of their daily rounds.

Because I usually stayed with Jennifer, these men and women most often found her nestled in my arms, with Don at his General Motors job, and an increasingly bewildered Holly, not yet old enough to spend her days at school, entrusted to one grandmother or another. They sometimes asked me questions and other times talked among themselves as if Jennifer and I couldn't hear, their whispers traveling in circles.

See here, what the nervous system is capable of, how

she trembles for hours on the verge of a febrile seizure but doesn't seize? Touch this limb, feel the elasticity in the tendons and muscles, how the joint doubles back on itself? Listen to the heart, do you hear the murmur that comes and goes? Consider this X-ray: where is the right kidney?

One morning, when she was still under a year old, a cluster of doctors from across Michigan, at St. Joe's for a meeting, gathered around her to see, for the first time in their experience, a person with suspected but not yet confirmed Rubinstein-Taybi Syndrome. Some tried to hide their fascination beneath layers of professionalism, while others, less subtle, peered down on Jennifer and tweaked her. Among them were those who shrugged their shoulders, stumped, and those who had seen it misdiagnosed as Down Syndrome elsewhere. There was even one specialist, memorable in his crisp navy blue suit, his pocketed hand, and his gambler's flair.

"If I were a betting man," he said, "I'd lay my money on Rubinstein-Taybi." He flitted in and out of the hospital room just long enough to set my heart and mind racing.

"Medicine isn't a perfect science," Dr. O'Neill told me later, when I expressed my confusion. His words felt like a scolding. "We'll have to watch and see how she develops."

I couldn't imagine how her development might clear up the puzzle of her condition – it wasn't like she was going to grow new parts – and, being a young mother with little more than a hit-and-miss emergency room education, I didn't know to push for advanced testing.

I'll have to wait, I concluded, for some professional to share his epiphany. And so I waited. Don was my devoted shadow.

Jennifer's traits constituted an ambiguous brew, Dr. O'Neill said. The thumbs and toes, the eyes and nose, could mean many things – Rubinstein-Taybi Syndrome most likely, but possibly the similar Cornelia De Lange Syndrome, or Turner Syndrome, or even a variation on the exotic sounding, but frightening, Bird-headed Dwarf of Seckel Syndrome.

More than not wanting Jennifer to have a tail, I did not want her to have a bird head. But, was her face an optical illusion? Did it slant away from that nose? Did her forehead protrude? Did her eyes long to be spread to the outer reaches of her brow? Were these qualities going to become more apparent as she grew? Was there something wrong with me that I couldn't see an eagle or a crow or a sparrow, trying to free itself from beneath my daughter's skin?

I looked down on her, my thoughts tracing a bizarre path backward in time. They filtered in and out of events in my own childhood, until they landed at last on the yellow Three Stooges ring I purchased from a gum machine and placed on my eight-year-old finger. Back then, I tried to specifically move the ring finger without moving the others, but I lacked the muscle control to do so. Either the ring finger stalled stiffly all by itself, or the pinky and middle fingers lurched along with it.

So did Curly Howard. Embossed there on the cover of the ring, his face was a starburst optical illusion – tilt my fingers and ring one way and Curly displayed mock surprise, as if Moe Howard were posed beside me, ready to throw him a slap. Tilt my fingers and ring the other way, and Curly's face relaxed into a nyuk-nyuk half smile. If I drummed my fingers over and over, Curly's mock surprise relaxed back and forth, back and forth.

Jennifer rested on my lap the way my fingers did when I was a child – warm flesh against warm flesh, comfortable but the focus of my curiosity. I studied her face the way I had studied that ring, tried to fathom her mysteries, held her gently at her sides with my extended hands. I tilted her as I tilted the ring, oh so subtly, from side to side, half expecting her *coo* to change to a *tweet*. She looked at me, her dark eyes trying to focus, her nose standing out like the arm on the face of a sundial.

I wondered, Bird-headed Dwarf of Seckel, are you there inside my daughter? The name mesmerized me in all that it implied – its blend of the exotic, of magic and trepidation.

Against my knee, between my hands, Jennifer rocked this way and that. My imagination rocked this way and that with her. Yes, I had to admit it. I could see what Dr. O'Neill saw – the way her nose suggested a beak. It was as hooked as a parrot's. I could see the way her forehead and tiny mouth and simple chin created an effect too, especially since she had not yet sprouted teeth.

Her eyes may or may not have wanted to be a bird's. There was a faint downward slope to the sockets, but they faced forward, nonetheless. And while there was not even the slightest hint that they wanted someday to align themselves along the sides of her head, the eyeballs moved almost independently. They drifted back and forth, up and down, on the whims of the immature muscles that worked them. Jennifer was unable to control them, but I could see that she was trying. She wanted to see me truly, as I wanted to see the real her. There was a slight tremor to her head. She had solicited the help of her neck muscles in her effort. That was how hard she was trying. That was the level of her infant concentration.

I could imagine all sorts of futures for a girl who shared flesh with a bird. Oh, I embarrass myself, but I could see her excelling in a children's bob-for-apples game over Halloween. A tendency to bob her head would be as natural to her as the ready-made costume of deformity. I could see her scratching the earth with her bare toes in summer. I could see her getting her feathers ruffled. Having flights of fancy. Sprouting wings and taking off! I could hear her song trailing back and back.

A few months after Jennifer's birth I would see a Bird-headed Dwarf in the emergency room, and have my fears about that particular syndrome put to rest.

He was one of two Bird-headed Dwarfs, brothers, who

were occasional patients in the ER, usually on the midnight shift. St. Joe's was a teaching hospital located in a working class community, and I had heard rumors of them periodically, so remarkable was their condition that it generated conversation, but I had never encountered the brothers before. On this day, their mother appeared in the early afternoon, her face haggard from years of worry, the younger brother in a blanket in her arms.

"Michael is very sick," she said, bouncing him up and down slightly, like a mother soothing a fretting infant, as she stepped up to the admitting desk.

I stood off to the side of the office, next to a coworker who was seated at the typewriter. "Name, address, age," came Mary's questions, by rote. In the absence of triage nurses, our job included assessing a patient's desperation, taking billing information, creating a chart and ID bracelet, and notifying nurses if a patient seemed to be hemorrhaging, seriously ill, badly injured, or dead. We took turns at these tasks, sometimes energized by the relentless pace and variety of patients and their problems, sometimes grief-stricken by the human condition, sometimes amused at the ridiculous notions that constituted medical emergencies in people's minds such as facial scratches, head lice, or sexual escapades gone awry.

"… Twenty-six," came Michael's mother's response to the age question.

Mary looked at the blanketed bundle and blinked. "You mean twenty-six *months?*"

Michael's mother said, "No, twenty-six." She was impatient, worried, beyond explaining the unexplainable to the unenlightened, aloof in the invisible box she had erected around herself.

I remained silent and wrote Michael's name on a hospital identification bracelet, trying to be a non-presence in the palpable discomfort that filled the air.

"But …," Mary continued, innocently.

Another clerk, Henrietta, whose back had been turned to these goings-on, suddenly recognized the mother's voice, intuiting the problem at that very moment, and she pivoted and interjected, "Michael is twenty six."

Henrietta's four words implied this:

That bundle is not a baby, it's a twenty-six-year-old man, and I've seen him before on the midnight shift, as well as his equally small brother who died last year at age twenty-eight, and the mother knows what she's talking about, and you'd better shut up now before you really put your foot in your mouth.

Mary silenced herself, like a guilty child trapped in the glare of an angry adult, while Henrietta summoned a nurse. I walked back to the examining room to slip the ID bracelet on Michael's ankle.

His mother laid him on the table gently, and she opened his blanket to expose the most fragile, tiny human being I had ever seen. I had to stifle a gasp. Michael was scarcely longer than my forearm and not as big around. He couldn't have weighed more than six pounds. "Come on, Michael," she said, pleading the life into him. "Hang on, Michael, hang on."

Michael did, indeed, look like a bird – a delicate, white cockatiel that had fallen from its nest and landed on its back. His arms and legs were drawn up before him, claw-like, the fingers working independently to grasp the air. His thin hair, in white wisps, fell over his tiny forehead like a feathered crest. Michael's chest expanded and fell, trying to take in shallow, laborious breaths.

"Come on, Michael," his mother cooed, as I cautiously stepped forward and slipped the orange ID bracelet onto his ankle. I felt like a misplaced forester banding the rarest bird of all.

While fearing the Bird-headed Dwarf of Seckel Syndrome, I clung to the possibility – what seemed to me the relative safety – of Turner Syndrome for a while. Jennifer could, Dr. O'Neill had suggested, have a mosaic form.

Mosaic. There was a word that in its implied beauty I could appreciate. It sounded lovely, and I could not help but picture a ceramic mosaic, specifically an icon of the Virgin Mary, for some reason – tiny broken tiles of deep blues and reds and golds and browns, in a circle, with Mary in its center observing a candle in her hand, lovingly, the way she must have observed her own baby.

Dr. O'Neill had told me there was a woman who worked as a lab technician in the hospital where Jennifer was born – a different hospital from where I worked – who had Turner Syndrome. He mentioned her name off-handedly, and I remembered her from high school, but did not tell him. She was a teenaged friend of my sister, and I had reminded her of this fact when she drew blood from me in the recovery room. She and I had laughed over the coincidence. This woman was short and pixie-like, as perky and bright as the actress Mary Martin when she played Peter Pan. I would not have guessed, during all those years, that she wasn't perfect.

"Turner Syndrome," Dr. O'Neill said, "affects only females. They have one chromosome." And that is all. One X. They are sterile, short, of normal intelligence. "She leads a perfectly normal life. She's married, has children." He paused, recognized his mistake and modified his encouragement. "Er, no, she can't have children."

Normal intelligence. There is something to hope for, I told myself, rolling these words around in my mouth like chocolate morsels. They were enough to perpetuate my denial about Jennifer's limitations and to launch me on a mission. That I worked in the emergency room, where I had access to medical information and various specialists, seemed an optimum opportunity to me. Subsequently, I began to seek information at every turn. I perused medical book after medical book on my dinner breaks. I picked nurse brains, piece-by-piece, deformity-by-deformity. I stopped doctors in the hall.

I approached one particular gynecology resident as if he were a long lost friend. A Sikh, he was statuesque and elegant, prince-like. I was aware, because I had overheard their gossip, that many nurses made love to him in their workaday fantasies, or in their nighttime dreams. What I wanted from him was something infinitely more impossible. I wanted an answer.

Dr. Singh wore a beard and a turban, and he treated patients on the gynecology and obstetrics wards, as well as in the emergency room, when need be. During my pregnancy with Jennifer, there'd been days when he'd rubbed my belly for luck, like a tourist in a gift shop might rub a statue of the Buddha's, and he'd asked, "How are we doing?"

He seemed accessible to me, so kind and genuinely interested. This educated, lovely man will know about Turner Syndrome, I thought. And so I went to him, gingerly, with a soft voice – "It is possible that my baby daughter has Turner Syndrome."

He seemed shocked, but he listened, following my train of thought.

"If she does, Dr. O'Neill says she might be a 'mosaic'. Can you explain what that means?"

He had an answer ready in his head. "It means she would have both male and female traits. Testicles in her abdomen."

I took in a huge gasp. I inflated with it. It was so big I thought I might fly down the hospital corridor and bang against walls. As I exhaled, I wanted to self-propel and annihilate every doctor I encountered.

"What!" I gasped again.

Carolyn H. Walker

Someone interrupted us before I could insist on an explanation, and I was left alone to dwell on this concept. Instead of offering peace of mind, Dr. Singh's definition reinforced my anxiety. It snuggled in close and by the end of my shift I had cursed and cursed my curiosity. I cursed myself for asking – and especially for choosing to ask someone other than Dr. O'Neill.

Hysteria

If you would take your right hand and turn the palm upward with the fingers un-fanned and the thumb slightly extended, I would show you how to locate Clarkston, for as any Michigander knows, a right hand mimics a map of the mitten-shaped Michigan perfectly well. Clarkston is there, about midway down on the fatty mound of flesh, west of your thumb and southeast of what is known in palmistry as the Line of Life. On a palm that isn't marred by scars or blemishes, the Line of Life, for a distance, vaguely follows the path of I-75, a six-lane interstate that touches Clarkston along its northern-most boundary.

Clarkston is a place with a lovely reputation, earned through its community spirit, historic houses, small park, quaint shops, scattered churches, bar/restaurants, grocery market, service station, antique store, and friendly people. By the time of our 1977 move there, Dr. O'Neill had long been a fixture in the area, where he both lived and worked, often treating patients at no charge, answering the phone at all hours, opening his office on Sunday afternoons, and making house calls after the fashion of old-time country doctors.

He was much beloved by almost everyone, and took on a sort of mythic status, so much so that a downtown restaurant had a hamburger on its menu called The O'Neillburger. Dr. O'Neill was often the subject of over-the-fence musings, card club conversations, and general gossip.

Once, while in St. Joe's cafeteria, I eavesdropped while a nurse told others at her table that she'd heard Dr. O'Neill brought a boy back to life after another physician had declared him dead. Her listeners leaned toward her enthralled, they tittered and chirped. Their body language indicated they believed what she was saying, like this kind of heroism on the part of Dr. O'Neill was not only plausible, but likely.

As the mother of a child with unfolding, seemingly bottomless health issues, I wanted Dr. O'Neill to be a miracle worker. I wanted him to cure Jennifer.

I wanted to ask him if what the nurse had said was true, but I never summoned the nerve. Instead, I made up a high-drama scenario in my mind – an accident on the interstate near his farm, a boy flung from the front seat of his mother's car and sprawled out on the pavement, an anonymous doctor stopping to help but finding he's too late. He stands away from the child and tells the mother, the crowd, there is no hope. The mother wails.

But wait! Here comes Dr. O'Neill, charging across a field in his lab coat. There he is, kneeling over the child, moving his hands, murmuring. There is the boy with his eyelids fluttering, his chest rising. There is Dr. O'Neill helping him to his feet. There is the sound of cheering.

All that was good or bad, happy or sad, right or wrong in our life converged after Don and I moved our daughters from East Sheffield Street into a new ranch house. Holly was four years old, Jennifer six months and not yet diagnosed, when we undertook our move during a winter storm.

Beset by the medical expenses that accompanied Jennifer, Don worked more and more hours to keep up with them, while I took on a melancholy. I became increasingly afraid of our neighborhood and the dysfunctional people who occupied it. Our home was filled with worry about Jennifer, and was a constant, sad reminder of the lost Matthew. In addition, Holly was nearing school age and I wanted her to attend a good elementary school, not the ho-hum one she was destined for. I urged Don to move for several months, and he finally agreed.

Joy had told me of a new subdivision in Clarkston that she and her husband had looked into, and Don and I went to investigate it on a sunny spring morning.

I had heritage in Clarkston, which made it even more appealing to me. It was where my mother's parents had farmed in the early 1920s, and where my mother was born.

When I was little, our family had enjoyed Sunday drives to the Clarkston area, during which Mom regaled us with her earliest memories. She pointed out the site of her girlhood home, the church and school she attended, and shared those experiences that came floating randomly into her mind – riding her horse Merry Legs, shoving a banana down her brother's throat, splitting her finger into two halves in a wringer washer, the way Clarkston's then-doctor had saved it by wrapping the halves together, and how he treated her morale with bits of candy.

At seven or eight years old, riding in the backseat of the car, I found Mom's little adventures thrilling and funny, and begged to hear more. I listened to the swing of her voice, lowered the window to let the air ruffle my hair, and watched while fields of corn and hay and apple trees flew by. I'm sure this was where and how I acquired my love of stories, and of the village that I would one day call home where I would write them.

Don and I contracted with the builder and had the excitement of picking out cupboards and flooring and light fixtures. Periodically, we drove over and strolled around the lot, around the poplar that would someday hold up a tire swing, and discussed flowers and sod and our impending happiness.

By mid-December the house was ready for us, and I was determined we would spend the holidays there. On moving day, Don and I sent our daughters off to my grandmother's for the night, loaded our furnishings and our fully-decorated Christmas tree into a U-Haul truck, and transported the whole of it to our new home while snow fell. Against the soft glow of streetlights and the dark of night, it was like we were moving inside a snow globe. I was euphoric. What I didn't anticipate was that I would take the doom with me. Several months after our move, my emotions flooded out of me, triggered by, of all things, a birthday gift.

Mother had meant well when she extended it toward me, its flat rectangular shape wrapped in colorful paper. The gift was meant to be a surprise, but I knew instinctively what she'd done. She'd purchased the framed painting I'd admired during our June shopping spree, when she and I took a day to shop for baby clothes and poke around stores we'd never investigated before. I thought the painting surreal and fanciful, the kind of art I liked, and exclaimed over it in the shop. It featured several horses, white as kid gloves, and they sprouted wings as they went around on a carousel, then flew off, one Pegasus after another, disappearing into the night sky. In the lower right hand corner stood a round-eyed little girl with brown braids, of maybe five or six years, looking as if her heart would break if she had to leave this mystical place. She reminded me of Holly.

The weather on the day of our shopping spree was lovely and we ambled along, carefree, with Holly walking beside me, and Jennifer, now eleven months old, in her stroller. We ate lunch out. We visited and laughed.

A bit later, as she'd done for holidays and birthdays my

entire life, my mother went into magic fairy mode. She drove an hour north of her home, retraced our steps into the art gallery, and paid nearly $100 for the painting. Then she took it home and kept it a secret, anticipating I would show delight on my twenty-eighth birthday in September.

When she handed it to me, I feigned the excitement I knew she was hoping for. "You bought it!" I said. The "bought it" was fear dressed up as glee, but Mother didn't seem to notice. Instead, she stood across from me and grinned.

The months since Jennifer's birth had swept one into another like shifting storm clouds, and I had become caught up in them, shrouded in their uncertainties, consumed by their demands, unable to see anything with clarity.

Weeks before my birthday, thoughts of the painting had begun weighing on my mind. I grew increasingly and inexplicably afraid Mother had bought it for me. I sensed she had, but tried to push that intuition away. In my imagination, the painting had morphed from a symbol of fun to something sinister that evoked terror in me.

As I took the package, my insides heaved and tried to come up into my throat. Mother watched as I pulled the wrapping away and looked. The horses were in the act of abandonment. The little girl's expression had changed. She was no longer dismayed that the fair was about to close. She no longer sought one last ride. She was lost. No, forgotten. No, no, she knew something. Her eyes peered out, caught mine, told me what she knew. *You can't have this painting. If you keep it, something bad is going to happen to Holly.* It was a completely irrational thought, a superstition born of my anxiety. I knew this, but it put down roots and overwhelmed me.

I said goodbye to Mother, loaded the painting into the trunk and slammed the lid on it. Then I drove by Joy's, took it out in her driveway, and, feeling both silly and nervous, asked, "What do you think of this painting?" I hoped she would ease my mind, but she didn't.

I don't know if Joy saw something in my face, or heard something in my voice, or if she truly shared my intuitions, but she said, "It looks like someone is going to die." Her eyes went from the painting to me and then back to the painting again.

That was all it took. I felt the ker-thunk of an adrenaline-driven heart. I said goodbye to her and slammed the painting into the trunk again. When I got home I propped it against an empty dining room wall, knowing I could never hang it. Knowing I couldn't face that little girl, day in and day out. I had to get rid of the painting, and soon.

But how, I thought, am I going to explain this to Mother? I knew I would sound unreasonable, but my fear was too strong. I was compelled by it. I picked up the phone and dialed her, struggling for words when she said hello. "Mom, I have to take the painting back. I can't keep it."

I could tell from her tone that she was flabbergasted. "But, but, Carolyn, I thought you liked that painting," she stammered.

"I did. I'm sorry, but I just can't keep it. I have to take it back. It scares me."

An awkward silence came between us. I was embarrassed but determined and repeated myself once more. "I just can't keep it. I have to take it back." I can't remember if I invoked the worry I had for Holly as I spoke to her. It was hard to expose my vulnerability to my mother in this way. I burst into tears.

"Well, all right," she finally said.

We disconnected and I went to the basement to throw a load of clothing into the washing machine. Crossing the basement's floor, I slipped on a nightgown in my path. I laundry surfed on a silken wave, fell to my right knee, and then onto my hip, and finally onto my elbow and shoulder. I gave in fully to the wave's pull, collapsing with a limpness like that of the garments in the pile. Lying there, surrounded by Don's work shirts and Jennifer's sleepers and Holly's school clothes and my blouses and underwear, I put my hands to my face and released my accumulated anguish. When I was spent, exhausted, I went upstairs to the kitchen and explained my fears to Don, who whether he understood or not, at least came across as compassionate, for which I was immensely grateful.

"Well, if that's what you have to do ..." He didn't turn away from the sandwich he was making.

I returned the painting to a tolerant gallery owner who agreed to an exchange but wouldn't give my mother's money back. I didn't want a replacement because I didn't want a reminder with its echo-like potential to stir my anxiety at a future time, but left with no choice except to waste my mother's money completely, I traded it for a slightly larger abstract of blues and blacks and reds. Colors and lines and random shapes splashed all over the canvas. I hung it above the stairs that led to our family room. It hung there lifeless and useless and unappreciated for the decade we lived on Foxchase Lane, where it became encrusted by dust and the smoky residue of Don's cigarettes. I went up and down the stairs, passed it day in and day out, with little more than a glance, the same way I passed strangers on the street.

Freak Show

At long last, after all the months of self-induced agony – my imagination ever the victor – one of the doctors had a brainstorm. We should bring Jennifer, not yet a year old, to an upcoming symposium of doctors, a meeting of the minds, a gathering of specialists who might be able to collectively discern what exactly it was that had overtaken her. The symposium, to be held at St. Joe's, was to be led by a prominent growth and development specialist from Children's Hospital of Michigan, a codger named Dr. Smalley who, it turned out, had the wisdom, appearance, and presence of Winston Churchill.

If Don and I agreed to participate, we might further not only our own knowledge, but medical knowledge in the broad sense. We might dispense the benefit of our experience across this consortium to other patients and families we would never know.

Craving answers even as we dreaded them, Don and I agreed. We did the best we knew to do by way of preparation. We dressed in our good clothes, bundled Jennifer up in a cute outfit, and entered the auditorium, a large measure of awkwardness in our wake.

I knew that none of us should feel like sideshow freaks when we climbed onto the stage, but that was nevertheless how I felt. Mounting the steps as someone darkened the room, Don and I, with Jennifer in my arms, took seats between a brother and a sister who suffered from some form of obscure, familial gigantism, and another patient, an adorable toddler who had an unusual eye disability. My skin crept up my bones even as I told myself, "We're all human beings here. There's nothing to be afraid of."

If Don felt discomfort on a par with mine, he said nothing beyond that which could be conveyed by his darting eyes. He erected himself, an eyewitness in the folding chair next to mine, ramrod straight, typically silent, and probably overwhelmed. He acknowledged the doctors with a nod. We sat silently before the gathering of maybe sixty or seventy, and I looked from Don into the hovering face of the brother – a handsome face for all its chiseled enormity. We exchanged nods of acknowledgment but not words. I felt the penetrating stares of the doctors in the audience as they considered us, their curiosity tangible as they leaned forward and strained to improve their view. Dr. O'Neill's diamond-white head shone out from the middle of them. I was relieved that he was in attendance, our personal patron. His presence, for me a psychological tonic, helped to assuage my nervousness. I heard murmurs as the doctors, waiting for our introduction, conferred, their heads together in clutches of two or three.

Peculiarly, I also felt a kind of kinship with those in attendance. I had worked in the emergency room for nearly two years and by now had a good understanding of medicine and its terminology. I had a competency around body functions and blood and people in disarray. I found that the field of medicine energized me. I had also acquired a burgeoning respect for the countless maladies that can befall human beings. Very little surprised me anymore.

I recognized many, but not all, of the doctors and residents in the audience and was sure they recognized me as well. Some had worked around me in the ER, others had lined up alongside me in the cafeteria lunch line, and some had attended Jennifer on the pediatric floor. Others, physicians like Dr. Singh, had tolerated my increasingly intense questions when I stopped them, unsuspecting, to ask, "Is it significant when Jennifer's eyes jiggle in their sockets? Why does my daughter's urine smell like rotting fish?"

The occasional doctor volunteered, "Don't have any more children," as if Don and I were our own Frankenstein factory.

There was nothing conversational about the symposium. It was question-and-answer, and Don spoke only when he was addressed, while I assumed the lead and held forth with an abandonment that was driven by nerves. Don and I had already settled ourselves into the roles we would feel compelled to occupy for a lifetime – he the tireless unquestioning provider, me the emotional weight bearer and seeker. The observations that came out of the meeting shined like stars before me, each suggesting that maybe there were answers out there in the void.

Stage lights illuminated Jennifer on my lap as I began to field the doctors' questions.

"How old are you?"

"I'm twenty-seven and my husband is forty."

"How many pregnancies have you had?"

"Three."

"Were there any complications?"

"Not with Jennifer's pregnancy, but my first two resulted in premature births. The first child died."

"How is Jennifer's appetite?"

"Good."

"How much does she weigh?"

"Ten pounds."

"Do you plan to have any more children?"

(Long pause.)

"Being of sound mind and body, I do not."

(Sudden popcorn-like rattle of doctors laughing.)

I suffered from a shortsighted idealism when I said "yes" to Dr. Hague's post-symposium recommendation that Jennifer be photographed for educational purposes. A tall, bespectacled man with slicked, black hair and an air of supremacy, he placed a hand on my shoulder and peered down at me. "Take her to the hospital photographer. We should get her picture periodically, so we can study how she grows."

It wasn't enough for Dr. Hague, chief of pediatrics, that Dr. O'Neill would be monitoring Jennifer's growth during regular examinations. He wanted documentation. He wanted a piece of history. More competitive than the generous Dr. O'Neill, I sensed he wanted to have his say in the equation that would govern Jennifer's development, a prestige by proxy in her local fame and progress.

Even though I worked in the hospital, the only experience I'd had with its photographer had to do with getting my employee identification picture taken. A few days after Dr. Hague's request, Jennifer and I rode the elevator to the basement and began the trek down the lengthy, isolated corridor that led to the photography studio.

My steps into the photographer's room were slow and deliberate. It was as if I was walking into a turn-of-the-century daguerreotype, one in which it took many minutes to capture a single moment in time. I crossed the threshold, both wary and idealistic, a sleeping Jennifer in my arms, and grew mildly uncomfortable against the backdrop of basement walls, the single medical table and chair, and the scattered camera equipment. There was a peculiar absence of color in this dungeon of a room, a somberness in the sterile meld of black and gray and white, even as the skin on the photographer, Jennifer, and me lost its pink under the shimmering fluorescent lights. We were, all of us, anticipation-stiff, like mannequins, as the photographer considered the task before him.

What had he been told about us?

A young mother and her baby will come to you soon. The infant has rare birth defects. We want pictures of these.

The photographer, in white shirt, black pants and vinyl apron, was business-like when he greeted us. Methodical, lacking the passion and vision of a portrait artist, he stroked his chin nervously. He eyed his subject then lurched across the room to position a flash or two, on poles, beside the table. He wanted to cast the best light on things.

I watched with interest, filled with a mother's fervor about how the session should go. I could hold Jennifer, and he could zoom in on her sleeping face nestled against my breast. I could prop her against her blanket, a tiny toy in her hand, then stand behind the photographer and act the fool to coax a smile. Jennifer's pictures should be, I believed, Prettiest Baby Contest worthy. I wanted to tell the photographer, "Point your camera in a way that highlights the surprise hair, enhances the imp expression and captures her innocence." Instead he told me what to do.

"I want you to take all her clothes off."

"What? Take all her clothes off?"

"Yes."

"Even her diaper? You want me to take off her diaper? Here? But why?" My mind flooded and I heard myself grope for excuses. "It's cold in here. What if she pees?"

I was suddenly alarmed, and I felt like an unwitting accomplice in a perverse pursuit. I didn't want to strip my baby girl in front of a strange man, in front of a camera. I didn't want its lens, his eye, closing in on her vulnerabilities, her privacy. I didn't want to commit her deformities to an eternity on film. I was frozen in place, gripped in the expectations of this photographer, anonymous researchers, and a world of the medically curious.

"I want you to take her clothes off, and then I want you to stand her here." He was adamant. He gestured at the table, camera in hand, growing mildly impatient. "This won't take long. It's what the doctors want."

Doctors. Their authority permeated even this detached studio, infusing this man who did their bidding.

"But she can't stand up yet. She's too little. She can't stand up."

"Then you will have to hold her. Take her clothes off, and hold her here."

I scrambled Jennifer out of her blanket and sleeper and diaper. I didn't want to do this, but I didn't know how to stop the process. I didn't know how to say *no*. I wrapped my arms and hands around her naked body. I pressed the blanket in front of her.

"Stand her here."

I obeyed, reaching around from behind her and scooping her onto my forearm. Her legs and feet, too new and unable to bear her scant weight, could not support her. I placed her on the table in front of me, my forearm like a closet rod holding her up from beneath her arms. Her neck muscles were lax, her head drifted to one shoulder. I felt sick to my stomach. This isn't what mothers of babies do, is it?

The photographer stepped back and tilted his head this way and that. "Spread her legs," he said.

"Spread her legs? But why?"

"The doctors will want to see everything." He nudged her feet apart, told me to move my arm and grip her by the hands, then pull her arms above her head and away from one another. He wanted her upright and spread-eagled.

"But …"

He stepped out into the hall and called across it for assistance. An automaton in a white lab coat appeared. He mumbled to her and she took Jennifer from me. Suddenly my baby became a chicken carcass just out of its plastic wrapping, trunk protruding, wing tips held aloft, drumsticks scraping the table.

I moved around and behind the photographer to see what his camera saw, capturing the image forever – my baby with wide eyes and an equally wide mouth that wanted so much to cry out, *But, Mama, why?*

The photographer's camera shutter staccato-fired. He lowered the camera, rewound the film, and spoke. "The doctors will want us to do this once every six months or so for a while, and then once a year while she grows."

I looked at the floor, wanting to weep. "Will these pictures go in a book somewhere?" I asked him. I remembered the adolescent I saw in the medical book on the morning after Jennifer's birth. I understood now why she looked like a caricature. I wondered if anybody, anywhere, ever, could benefit from photographs of a spread-eagled baby. The photographer shrugged and said he wasn't sure. Then he left the room while I put Jennifer back in her clothes. I encased her in her blanket and clutched her close. I was like a thief in the way I hurried her from the studio.

I still do not know why Don and I were put through over a year of agonizing when some relatively simple genetic studies might have eased at least some of our fears. True, Rubinstein-Taybi Syndrome had no known cause at the time and could not have been detected by tests, but Turner Syndrome, at least, might have been ruled out. It was likely Dr. O'Neill didn't realize the impact of his musings on my imagination. He couldn't have known that I brooded, that I took his words and those of the other doctors, and wrestled them like I might a life-or-death crossword puzzle. He couldn't have known that once I became exhausted from the wrestling, I flung the words into the air and juggled them with Don, whose guesswork was no better than mine.

Our introduction to Dr. Smalley – the development specialist from Children's Hospital of Michigan who had led the symposium at St. Joe's – proved to be a fortuitous one. A kindly, savvy physician with generations of experience behind him, he invited us to bring Jennifer to Children's Hospital for a state-of-the-art evaluation, an invitation Don and I readily accepted. It took a few months for us to get an appointment and by the time we went Jennifer was over a year old.

His office, set deep in a maze of book and instrument filled rooms, was resplendent with his competence, medical tomes lining the walls, a simple overhead light all that was needed to illuminate it. Entering it, Don and I felt the presence of answers, tangible as this man's authority. We walked in reverently, humbly, as if we were walking into the Holy of Holies.

Jennifer was put through a gentle but efficient manhandling. She was flipped and turned like a fish being trussed for market. The circumference of her head and the length of her torso and extremities were measured with a measuring tape, the zing of its spring echoing up from his well-practiced hands as Dr. Smalley stretched and closed it. He darkened his room and peered so deeply into her eyes that I thought he most certainly saw her soul. He tapped her little rock knees and the pads of her feet for reflexes. He listened to her heart and lungs, his head angled, his eyes studying the office walls while his ears listened for clues, like those of a rescuer trying to fathom life at the scene of a disaster. He peeked in her ears, pulling the flaps of them away from her head with his finger and thumb. He ran his liver-spotted fingers across the span of her fontanel. He murmured under his breath against the backdrop of my rambling, "Could she have *both* Turner and Rubinstein-Taybi syndromes?"

Clinical syndromes such as Rubinstein-Taybi, we would learn that day, cannot be established through genetic or blood or any other formal studies. They are, instead, diagnosed visually and somewhat intuitively, the diagnosis being based on a composite of characteristics. Nevertheless, in an effort to rule out that which he could rule out, Dr. Smalley ordered a chromosome study and a buccal smear, a scraping of the mucosal lining of Jennifer's mouth, the cells of which would indicate her spot on the curve of humanity and its associated sexuality. I held her on my lap while he produced a tiny wooden spatula that was not unlike a Popsicle stick, urged it between her lips and gums, and pressed its edge along the inside of her cheek. Beneath her skin, I could see the bulge of it buffing off a layer of Jennifer as efficiently as a nail file.

At our next visit a few months later, Dr. Smalley informed us that Jennifer was, at least on paper, a normal female. There were no deviations to her chromosome study or her buccal smear. Microscopically, it seemed, she was on a par with Cleopatra or Marie Curie or Queen Elizabeth or Holly or me.

I do not remember Don's response, but I remember mine. Sitting there across from the doctor, I hardly knew how to take in this news. That word *normal*, used finally in the context of our daughter, flew in the face of the obvious, now fifteen months old. It flew in the face of common sense. It flew in the face of Rubinstein-Taybi, looking with trust back at me.

On that day, when we left Dr. Smalley's office, I walked away from *normal* and all its simple promises, once and for all – just like I might have walked away from my sweater, had I neglected to lift it from the back of the chair on my way out the door.

I Looked There And Saw
Jennifer

A kernel of grace, a gem of it, was finally allotted after Dr. Smalley diagnosed Jennifer with Rubinstein-Taybi Syndrome. I do not recollect how the grace touched me at first or precisely when. I remember only the feelings that accompanied it – a perking of the senses and then an internal flooding, new knowledge carrying the potential to alleviate pain as well as cause it. I had been struggling as much against my frustration with doctors and their conspiracy of confusion as against fate, trying to come to terms with not only the syndrome but with its tentacle grip on our family. Rubinstein-Taybi had descended on us like an unwanted houseguest, and was here to stay.

My quest for knowledge, begun in those dabblings over medical dictionaries in the emergency room, had continued with a vengeance, often-thwarted research taking up much of what was left of my spare time. Don seemed to accept the changes Rubinstein-Taybi brought us matter-of-factly and without question, never varying from his routine, while I went from a desperate longing for a diagnosis, to an equally desperate longing to understand it. I went about my days as wife and mother, distracted, wrestling with my thoughts, trying to out-think doctors, looking for answers wherever I could find them.

Just as I cannot remember the actual moment when I learned there was a resource book, I cannot remember whether I learned of its existence by happenstance while on my job in the ER, or whether I spied some tidbit while poking around in a community library, or whether some medical secretary in a chain of medical secretaries blabbed her compassion when she was supposed to keep quiet, or whether some anonymous do-gooder voice tipped me off in a phone call. But this much was true – someone or something, somewhere, let it be known that the March of Dimes had a book about syndromes – and that this book would not be on some doctor's bookshelf, out of reach, deemed beyond my intellectual scope and emotional wellbeing. Nor would it be in a medical library, inaccessible to the general public, and thus to me. It would be where I could get my hands on it, where I could lay it across my lap and take my time studying pictures, memorizing terms, digesting information, causes. Discovering *why* Jennifer.

This book of syndromes became my Holy Grail as soon as I learned of it, and Dr. Jack Rubinstein, half of the Rubinstein and Taybi team, its champion.

Everything was gray when I drove to the March of Dimes office in the direction of Detroit. Or so it seemed. There was my inner turmoil, a swirl of angst and hope. There was my aging, dirtied phone book containing the charity's address on the seat beside me. There were the miles of rain-moistened, chuck-holed asphalt that stretched from my home to the office where the book shared space with other medical references.

I drove south, sure that Jennifer's doctors, even Dr. O'Neill, had one-by-one rationalized in their minds – so much is unknown, anyway, why talk of this with the child's mother? I detested more than anything those paternal physicians who put their hands on my shoulder and looked over their spectacles, saying most of what they had to say with their eyes. Believing they knew what was best for me. Believing ignorance was bliss. Was my mental and emotional struggle, my coupling of curiosity and fear, my need to know and understand, not as obvious as the calamity that had befallen Jennifer?

The book was a tome. The woman who handed it to me, gave me a chair to sit on, and she gave me privacy too, allowing solitude to fill the cramped, paper-strewn room where she had guided me. As distant telephones rang an accompaniment, I thumbed the book's pages, strummed them as I might a comb's teeth, summoning my nerve the way the infamous Pandora summoned her troubles, full of anticipation but afraid of what might greet me with the book's opening.

Though I had seen my share of broken, twisted bodies in the emergency room, I had not seen, aside from the Bird-headed Dwarf, the goodly portion of Mother Nature's frightening repertoire. I did not want my gaze to fall over the range of human horror, frozen in time and flattened on the page. Still, I knew I must face these images if I was to learn anything.

I opened the book, dared to peek at the title page which replicated the cover, and then at the table of contents. My stomach seized even at this. The names of various syndromes were set there in black-lettered rows against a backdrop of glossy white. The contents directed me to Rubinstein-Taybi Syndrome, a hundred pages or so in, and I quickly turned there, allowing the stagger of pages to slide and blur like so many shuffling cards. Gaping mouths and mismatched eyes and crooked ears and spots of hair and miniature heads and shriveled necks and hunched shoulders whirred past me with such speed that, appearing as one, they might have belonged to a single unfortunate soul.

The book finally fell open to Rubinstein-Taybi Syndrome,

and I saw there, on the right side, the same photograph of the adolescent girl I had pondered in the hospital book the morning after Jennifer's birth. Lacking any other identity, she had apparently become a poster girl for this disorder. Beneath her was a tribe picture – a clustering of seven or eight children with Rubinstein-Taybi Syndrome corralled from mental institutions and posed for this black-and-white photograph. Some were heavy-set and some were thin, some sat erect, others slouched. Arms and legs were askew and entangled, bodies were wedged together to fit the photographer's frame, eyes directed, as best as possible, toward the camera.

In their simple, unkempt variations, the children shared a common face, like those with Down Syndrome do. I looked there and I saw Jennifer, as she might have appeared had she been born a scant decade earlier, alive to an institutionalized existence, dead to all but the most meager hope.

The photographs were surrounded by print that told how Drs. Jack Rubinstein and Hooshang Taybi had described this syndrome from a smattering of patients they'd happened across in 1963. The article talked about some of the syndrome's manifestations – the signifying thumbs and toes, the facial features, the possibility of kidney and heart defects, the feeding and toileting obstacles, the tendency toward respiratory illnesses, the range of mental acuity, IQs from 29 to 70 or so. There was no information regarding cause, one of the things I most desperately wanted to know. Nor could I find whether Rubinstein and Taybi might attack our home or eventually our children's or grandchildren's homes at some other time.

Amid this pairing of print and conscience, this grasping for cause and effect, I noticed at the bottom of the page an address for Dr. Rubinstein, in Ohio. As I scratched it onto a torn piece of notebook paper, I dared to hazard the hope that he might still be alive and willing to talk. I composed my first letter to him, the first of years' worth, that afternoon at the kitchen table.

"Dear Dr. Rubinstein," I began, admitting the truth out loud to the kitchen walls – admitting the truth out loud for the first time – as I wrote, "My daughter has Rubinstein-Taybi Syndrome …"

The Eyes Have It

I joked with Dr. O'Neill's receptionist whenever I stepped up to her window, Jennifer on my hip – "I'd like to make a deposit." I was in his office so regularly now, once or twice a week on average, that I found myself handing money to her more often than to a bank teller. I'd pull $50 out of my coat pocket and slide it across the counter. She knew Jennifer and me by name, greeted us sheepishly, acknowledging the truth.

More truthfully, I was a financial go-between. There were times – most times – when due to Jennifer's tenuous health it was impossible for me to work outside our home and contribute to the family budget. I ended up quitting my job in the ER, and instead took evening classes part-time, finishing the English/ Journalism degree I'd abandoned when Don and I married, while Don punched a time clock six, or more often seven days a week. He would get up before the sun peeked over our neighborhood and, exhausted from his schedule, would return to bed when early darkness took its place.

Don's was a conveyor belt work ethic, set in motion by his mother, who had cared well into her adulthood for both her dying parents and several bachelor brothers before marrying a difficult man and taking up the task of making ends meet in their home.

I watched Don age, and grow more and more to look like his mother, as he toted the line she had handed off to him. Get up each morning, grab a sack lunch, quietly leave the house, arrive home at three o'clock, do some chores, eat, sleep. Get up each morning, grab a sack lunch, quietly leave the house, arrive home at three o'clock, do some chores, eat, sleep.

It takes a lot of money to raise a handicapped child and Don, committed to financial solvency in the face of Jennifer's medical expenses, remained resolute, shouldering his responsibility while perhaps finding solace in his predictable, comfortable world of tools and gears and blue-collar men – the predictable, comfortable world where he could fix things.

At 4 AM on most mornings, I'd lie in bed and feign sleep as he slapped the alarm button off, curled the blanket away from his chest, slinked fully out from under it and met the floor with a soft pounce. His pale skin took on the creamy yellow of the moonbeam that penetrated the window above our bed. His hair was hardly mussed. Not wanting to disturb me, he moved like a cat, silent on his feet.

He padded his way over to where he had folded his work clothes in a neat pile the night before, balanced alternately on one leg and then the other, and slipped first into his brown pants and then the tan shirt with the name *Don* embroidered in cursive loops on the left chest. I could make out his hands as they went through the motions of raising a zipper and closing buttons. He padded to the bureau – a dark brown monolith in the corner – and from on top of it, pocketed his wallet, comb, some loose change, his keys, and his employee ID badge.

I recognized these movements. His right hand went to one back buttock, his left hand to the other, then each hand to its respective hip. They slid down and slightly forward, and I heard the tinkle of change and keys as they plunked into place. Don then padded toward the bathroom and out of deference to me and our slumbering children waited until he had closed the door to flick on the light. I saw its beam creep in a yardstick line beneath the door, and shadows of his feet measure its length in shuffles as he prepared to shave.

I sometimes examined Don's ID picture when he was not in our room – thought about the Don who preceded me, saw him frozen in time on the job, his hair slicked back from his face, 1950's-Elvis style. His pompadour lay flat as a fallen cake, its long strands were swirled like icing trim around a French vanilla bald spot and then patted into place. He patted that hair like he might have patted a collie, just after he brushed it. The sides were stroked back once, twice, three times, first the left then the right. Then came the pat on top. He slid the butts of his palms along the edges of his temples, using the same gesture he had most surely mastered when he was a primping teen. The thumb and fingers of his right hand found the back of his head and pinched the tips of his hair into a thinning ducktail, and he patted that too.

In his ID photo, Don's black frame glasses were balanced a little off across his eye sockets, so that one eyebrow looked more prominent than the other. He held his head on a familiar angle, appearing like the proverbial emaciated convict.

If it was a summer's early morning as I lay in our bed and pondered Don, I would lay atop the sheet, either naked or skimpy night-gowned, and let the fan blow cooling air across my legs, my stomach, my breasts, my face. By mid-day, I knew, Don, an electrician, would have stood for hours, roasting and sweating on a beam near the ceiling of the plant. On hot days, the temperature climbed to roughly one hundred and twenty degrees inside the building, and the heat of course ascended. It was in this heat that he hung lights or connected machines with the current that ran them.

If it was winter, there was snow on the ground and ice thickening on the windshield of his car as he prepared to leave. I would pull the covers up close to my chin, shift my weight, and feel an oil-and-water mix of relief and guilt. I was glad I didn't have to get up at that hour and venture out into the cold. I marveled at his ability to do so, day in and day out for what would turn out to be forty years.

In the far distance of our kitchen, I could hear him striding his work boots across the floor, opening the refrigerator, wrinkling his sack lunch closed, turning the knob of the front door, pulling it gently behind him. Then I heard a long quiet, then the scrape of an ice brush cleaning the windshield, then the surge of the car's engine just before he eased it from the driveway. He waited until he had pulled onto the street and launched the car on its journey before he turned on the headlights, so they wouldn't bleed through a window and disturb the sleeping in our house.

I was only inside the General Motors automotive plant where Don worked once, during an open house in which I determined, perhaps wrongly, that the painted cement floors and giant machines had been cleaned of their grease and dust for show. Fancied up for company. I walked alone searching for Don among the assembly lines, under the overhead blocks, between the paint trucks, around the gizmos and wires, as foreign and curious in this setting as will be the first woman who treads the surface of Mars. I could smell in the air the metallic, oily odor he wore home, which seeped from his hair and scented his pillow at night. When I found him he was all smiles and pride and showman.

When he brought his paychecks home, the money went for bills – household, medical, dental, optical, orthopedic, physical therapy, speech therapy, and pharmaceutical.

It was in our bed that I finally felt safe speaking my fears about Jennifer's first surgery at age eleven months – an eye surgery, her first of what would be five eye surgeries. The day before the operation, I secretly went to a church sanctuary, where I got down on my knees in solitude and offered up an afternoon plea to God. *Please* ... Mine was a tip-of-the-iceberg prayer, though. My whispers, my begging, resonated through the empty chapel like the sound of a crack.

Fear seemed to have taken up permanent residence inside me. On the eve of this first surgery, it pressed itself out and spread like water, taking the shape of the air pocket that was between Don and me. He was to my right, so thin and angular that his form scarcely disturbed the flow of the blankets that draped us. I could see him out of the corner of my eye, looking something like a two-by-six with a head. I was certain that, like me, he was thinking about tomorrow. We were on our backs staring at the ceiling. We might have been viewing Michelangelo's painting in the Sistine Chapel we were so pensive and intense. Don radiated heat in my direction. It tempered me like a slow fire, sweated my concerns to the surface.

"Do you think Jennifer will be okay?" I asked, hoping that his intuitions would have more credibility than mine. He knew I needed reassurance, and offered some with his *yes*.

I had all kinds of nightmare scenarios circulating in my mind. I had created images of disaster, being less concerned about the actual cutting of her eye muscles to correct her cross eye than I was about the anesthesia that would render her immobile. I had no idea whether or not her system could tolerate anesthesia, or blood loss, or whether her surgeon might be prone to mistakes. I envisioned her spot-of-a-form on the operating table, the crowd of nurses and technicians encircling her in their green scrubs, all busy and efficient hands. Dr. Saul clamping her eyelids open in a vacant stare, posing his scalpel near a tear duct, inflicting the first stroke. Jennifer never flinching, never waking up.

"I would like us to pray together," I ventured softly, using words to that effect. Don and I were not accustomed to partnered prayers, and my request surfaced with a surprising amount of discomfort. I had to work up my nerve. Despite the fact that we had shared our meals, our bodies, our children, our home, and our lives all this time, I felt shy about this, like I was exposing some raw, vulnerable part of myself.

His face still aimed toward the ceiling, Don's voice came out of his mouth, a small geyser of agreement, "Okay". I felt his hand inch over and grope around to find mine and squeeze. I kept my prayer simple – "God, please let Jennifer's eye surgery go all right. Thank you, God. Amen."

After the surgery, Jennifer's eyes lined up correctly for a while, giving us a sample of what she might look like were her face closer to normal. However, the effects of the surgery were to be short lived, and soon her eyeballs, in their independence, rolled to the outsides of their sockets, a condition commonly known as "wall eye". If she'd had keen enough vision, she might have seen the sun rise and set on the two American coasts without ever adjusting her mid-western position.

"The problem is neurological. It arises in the brain," Dr. Saul told me when I expressed my frustration at this result. "It can only be corrected by treating the muscles."

Later, just before the fifth surgery when she was an adolescent, he said, "The best I can do is try to make her look cosmetically correct."

Still, as she aged, Jennifer managed to maintain a sense of humor through all of this and laughed whenever I asked her, close-up, as she attempted to study my face, "Which eye are you using to look at me?" This was a tease I could not resist. The very corners of her lids crinkled like an old lady's, and I noticed one eye – usually the right – suddenly align itself, a single lazy trouper snapping to attention.

Jennifer typically pulled a rubber face and focused that eye on me. Peering as it did from behind one orb of the eyeglasses which she wore from age three on, the eye had the appearance of a detective's in a magnifying glass. It was the color of a canned pea. The lid formed a slit and then expanded. She concentrated, took in my facial wrinkles and my scrutiny. We each stretched our cheeks down then tightened our lip and chin muscles to accommodate this near-sighted exchange.

"This one," she would say, pointing with her right index finger. She chuckled and deliberately leered. I inched even closer and observed that the eye quivered moderately. This trouper had a case of the nerves.

I always dreaded Jennifer's eye checkups, in part because I could see the bad news for myself, right there on her face, and in part because I knew each doctor visit was going to be akin to a cat's appearance in a birdhouse.

In addition to the surgeries, Dr. Saul had to measure her visual acuity – a monumental task due to her impulsivity, mischievous sense of humor, and all around lack of cooperation. She thought nothing of protracted, in-the-chair antics that included kicking him in the shins, arching her back, rolling her head, going limp or statue-posing, as well as assailing him with divergent, nonsensical conversations.

There was a brief period when, in his darkened examining room, she proudly displayed her emerging reading skills to Dr. Saul. As he summoned his patience and waited for her to pronounce the eye chart aloud, Jennifer aimed three fingers left or right, up or down, to mimic the direction of the E's mounted on the wall in the distance, or called out the letters she could see displayed through his eye machine. *A, A, A, A.* She loved that all the attention was on her, and could sense that I was beaming my encouragement from the shadows in a nearby chair, but over the years she grew bored with this routine.

"Oh, Jennifer," I coached, deepening my voice so it sounded like a mother bear's in a cave, "you know that you know your ABCs."

Splashing drops into her eyes, lurching to hit his target like a prizefighter, Dr. Saul got so he could match her rhythm, bob and weave, and make a diagnosis on Jennifer in less than half an hour. "OK, Jennifer," he echoed, "come on." It got so I could anticipate the exasperated twirl he would perform on his steel stool. She responded with a shrug and feigned ignorance, and Dr. Saul handed over a new prescription for glasses and scurried the *Jennifer Walker Traveling Trouble Act* over to the nearby optician's, where she picked out her frames like a child suddenly thrust into a candy shop. She considered the colors, touched and sniffed and tasted them, as if she were expecting a hint of peppermint or lemon.

Milestones Roll Uphill

Considering Jennifer's accomplishments from the perspective of her adulthood, and understanding that there are people with Rubinstein-Taybi Syndrome who are sentenced to lifetimes in which grunting and finger pointing constitute their primary modes of expression, I remind myself often, especially when my ears feel as if they might curl in upon themselves, that I should be grateful for Jennifer's accumulated, repetitive, constant, nonsensical routines – especially the routine about her adult-onset obsession, the *T-T-T-Titanic!*

"*T is for Tara, tickle, trombone, and ... T-T-T-Titanic!*" Jennifer likes to shout, her arms in the air like goal posts.

(*T is for turn the television off*, they might suggest, at least once in a while, on perpetually present *Sesame Street*. I can be a mimic, too. Hear me – "My favorite letter is S, as in *S is for stifle yourself! S is for silence is golden! S is for somebody hand me a muzzle! S is for stop it, already! I've heard enough*.")

I could not know that Jennifer would become a chatterbox and that I would someday long for silence when I placed her on the display table of a home decorating shop all those years ago, when she was nearing two, and she held forth with her first sort-of word, *Nah*. She flapped her arms vigorously, as she was increasingly wont to do, and said, for no other apparent reason than a simple delight in the fact that she could, *Nah, Nah, Nah, Nah, Nah, Nah*. As she said this, she stimulated a breeze that set wallpaper samples to fluttering.

"Kids," observed the store's proprietor, "*No* always seems to be their first word."

For several months I had wanted to believe that bursts of *Nah* meant Jennifer was finally trying to talk – even if she was saying *no*. Could *yes* be far behind? Could *boo-boo*? Could *please pass the milk*? Now I had the confirmation I longed for – a stranger's validation, gleaned with an untrained ear. I thanked him and on the way home considered the implications of this exchange, encouraged that she might soon learn to speak.

I believed in making good use of our time and taking advantage of Jennifer's attention span when I could capture it, essentially when she was in a position where she had to listen and talk with me. The most convenient times were when I was feeding her, or when she was learning to use the toilet, another skill that came late and only after a great deal of effort.

I lowered her into her highchair and while poking micro-mounds of mashed potatoes between her lips said, *Mmm, good*. Or I positioned her, when she was old enough, on the edge of the toilet seat and began with the word *careful*, concerned that due to her very small stature she might fall in.

"Careful," I told her. "Be careful." I watched her wobble back and forth like Humpty Dumpty on the wall then catch herself. She dipped her bottom down low into the toilet, settled, a jewel in its mounting.

When Jennifer was balanced safely, I sat myself on the bathtub lip, almost as precariously, my knees brushing hers on an angle. I knew a few words in the sign language of the deaf, words like *ball* and *cat,* which I'd mastered during the times I'd watched *Sesame Street* with her, and I signed these words to her and spoke them out loud as well. "Ba-a-ll. Ca-a-t."

I'd learned through trial and error that visual cues were an important component to teaching Jennifer. It was as if all five of her senses needed to be engaged in order for her to get the gist of even the simplest things.

Sometimes, to keep words and a context going, I read *Sesame Street* books to her as well. There was one in particular that featured simple words alongside photographs of a woman performing sign language.

Jennifer, of course, did not realize that what we were doing was work. She was delighted by this form of play. She loved the way she could make little whiskers with her fingers placed next to her grin and try to say *cat,* or the way she could round and then spread her hands big, as if to launch a beach ball from the toilet.

The first time Jennifer said *I love you* to me I focused on her, at rest on my lap, as if I were looking through a kaleidoscope. The living room around us faded to a warm and inviting amber brown – the color of the safe, quiet afternoon of her birth, and there was only Jennifer, crystalline before my eyes, surrounded by tiny sprays of yellow that highlighted her in the same way that gold highlights a goldstone.

She was small, maybe only the size of a two-year-old, but nevertheless a toddler of approximately four, or maybe even five years – much older than other children we knew who were learning to string words together. She had, with her jiggling eyes, been watching my face, and in particular my lips, for a very long time. I held her on my lap, where she fit so completely and so snuggly. We played pat-a-cake, we signed our words. I told her stories, I sang, and how she laughed! She underscored her enthusiasm by clapping, or sometimes flapping, her hands. Threw her head back in delighted squeals. Mouthed sounds, imitating, wanting to be like me.

I found this irresistible. I drew her against my chest and said, "I love you, Jennifer." Her body was warm and soft, her hair a silken handkerchief against my cheek. Mine was a long embrace. I could feel her as she breathed in and out against my breasts. I wanted to hug everything holy and healthy into her. I wanted the gift of a healing touch.

She pulled slightly away and began to form *I*, summoned it from inside her, tentatively, drew it out, tested the way it sounded, alone in the air. *I-I-I-I.* The *I* floated to my ears, perfect as a soprano's high C. She jiggle-watched for my reaction. I was all reaction, hovering expectantly, my demeanor and energy encouraging her. *Yes. Yes. Is there more?*

I felt the way hope set fire to my eyes, my cheeks, my lips. I echoed her *I* – implied in my tone, "You can do it." And she continued.

Jennifer's tongue, the tip of it slippery with saliva, fluttered over the noise of the letter *L*. Hers was a light flutter, a glossing of this difficult consonant. She was pleased with herself. *Uv oo* came next, two distinct, gentle hums from back in her throat. She paused as if she had practiced her timing, and then waited patiently for me. Her face queried, *Mama, do you understand what I have said to you?*

I let myself fall into her words with such utter, utter, abandonment.

Sometimes from the vantage point of hindsight, I think it was a good thing that we didn't know what to expect from Rubinstein-Taybi Syndrome during Jennifer's developmental years. It never occurred to us that there were others like her who would never walk or talk or read or socialize, or that Jennifer might suffer such a fate.

Believing Dr. O'Neill's prediction that she would be slow to reach her milestones but that she would nevertheless reach them, Don and I simply assumed she was going to be delayed and we did what we could to nurture her along in the same ways we had nurtured Holly. We read *Sesame Street* and *Disney* books to her, entertained her with music, took her for walks in her stroller, and played games with her, particularly one, *The Flop*, which we invented quite by accident when we were teaching her to walk.

Jennifer's feet were configured so that her toes and the balls of her feet pointed outward and her arches rolled in. With short, plump, legs, she looked a bit like a penguin, standing not on the soles of her feet, but on her ankle bones, teetering, her belly rounded forward, her butt pushed out. Like most babies, she taught herself to pull up and stand at the furniture – her sturdy, strange toes pressing furiously into the floor to stabilize her, her chin resting on the seats of the chairs – but walking itself was extremely difficult for her. The necessary body parts and their coordination went in too many of the wrong directions.

Don, Holly and I eventually coaxed Jennifer into a walk, at about age three, by playfully passing her around an increasingly large circle after dinner. Inevitably, the circle got large enough that it was a stretch for Jennifer to make it from one of us to another. We would send her off on her wobbly legs, her head and shoulders pitched forward, and when it appeared she was going to fall, the receiving person would reach to catch her while exclaiming an exaggerated *Fl-o-o-oppp,* with an enthusiastic, undulating voice. Jennifer loved our undivided attention and the silliness of our exclamations and within months she was not only walking but performing a sort of gallop, skills she would lose only a few years later, when birth defects in her left knee, now hidden, would overwhelm her.

In addition to the games we played, I surrounded Jennifer as best I could with friends, including a stint in a mother-and-tot program, where I urged her to use the slides, the pull toys, and the tiny jungle gyms, catching her when she fell, noticing that even at this tender age, before any of them had real language, "normal" children could sense she was different. Jennifer and I tolerated their stares for a full semester before Jennifer found her comfort zone elsewhere.

When she was a little over two years old, during one of the hospitalizations that punctuated this period, someone informed me that Michigan law mandates educational opportunities for children with disabilities from birth through age twenty-six years, the belief being that early intervention helps to give them advantages and a more promising outlook. As a result, I placed my first phone call to our community school network, and soon after Jennifer was evaluated by a psychologist and a speech therapist who came to our house bearing balls and dolls, psychological tests disguised as games, assessment forms, notebooks, optimism, and a hint of promise – and she was enrolled in an enrichment program for disabled toddlers.

Some fifteen miles from our home, the program was the closest to offer the intense physical and mental stimulation that Jennifer needed, the two women explained. There, they would work on skills like talking, walking, drinking from a straw, eating with silverware, and using the toilet.

Because there were no programs dealing exclusively with mental retardation for that age group, she was placed into a "Physically or Otherwise Health Impaired (POHI)" classroom with other variously challenged toddlers. Programs of this nature, called "center programs," drew their students from an array of local communities, since rarely were there enough disabled children needing the same type of help, at the same age, in a single school district.

A few days before Jennifer began attending, Pat, the psychologist, picked us up at home and drove us for a preliminary visit. Jennifer rode along clueless in her car seat while I found myself troubled by increasing trepidation and wondering in what ways the other children would be disabled. Finally, as we rounded a curve and the school came into view, a question tumbled out, compulsive and embarrassing, betraying my misgivings and my ignorance.

"What kind of children will we see when we get there?" I asked Pat. I was afraid Jennifer would be repulsed … no, I was afraid I would be repulsed.

But there was only one child whose deformities unnerved me, a towhead named Frank, who had an upper jaw like a great white shark and fingerless/toeless hands and feet shaped like lobster claws. He sidled up to Jennifer, his eyes smiling above his shark mouth as the teacher welcomed us and gave my daughter a cymbal and drumstick, instruments with which the brood of six or eight children – children with Down Syndrome, blindness, cerebral palsy, and so on – had already been equipped.

Jennifer seemed to have an immediate affinity for Frank who, Pat told me, participated in this program so that he could grow comfortable being seen in public. I seemed to be the only person in the room who was conspicuously aware of him, and as soon as she spoke I was struck by the notion that Frank's education was geared at teaching him how to accept the stares of others. I felt shame creep up my cheeks in the form of a deep and burning blush.

The teacher ticked on a record player and I observed with surprise that even though she could not yet walk, Jennifer had it in her to dance. She and Frank, now seated, bounced their torsos in counter-rhythm, like two pistons without a care in the world. She mimicked Frank and flapped her arms so that her drumstick twanged her cymbal. Totally entranced, Jennifer failed to notice when I left the room so Pat could drive me home. In the midst of all this, what I failed to notice was how readily my daughter could get along without me.

The week following our first visit to the POHI class, after the necessary paperwork had been completed, I put Jennifer on a yellow school bus for the half hour ride to school. She was still in diapers, which meant I had to pack her with full baby regalia. I handed her, her diaper bag, and her baby bottle up to the bus driver for the first time and prayed for her protection as the bus pulled out of our driveway, my eyes lingering on it, her safety completely dependent on the competence and compassion of strangers. I watched the bus round the curve in our street and go out of sight. I imagined Jennifer inside it, so short she couldn't see over the seat in front of her, bobbing along, accepting this turn of events as easily as she would have accepted a trip to the park.

What I couldn't know as I relinquished her this first time was that the scenario would repeat itself, virtually unchanged, for the next twenty-four years, the exception being that Jennifer, at age five, would finally outgrow the need for a diaper bag and a bottle.

The program paid huge dividends for her, and within six months she learned to feed herself with a spoon, drink from a straw, and speak nearly sixty words, up from the six she spoke – *mama, daddy, yes, no, ball, cat* – when she began school.

At the same time, I found myself learning a new language as well. It was a language of acronyms – Physically or Otherwise Health Impaired (POHI), Individual Education Planning Committee (IEPC), Trainable Mentally Impaired (TMI), Educable Mentally Impaired (EMI), Severely Multiply Impaired (SXI), Occupational Therapy (OT), Physical Therapy (PT), Community Mental Health (CMH), Association for Retarded Citizens (ARC), Macomb Oakland Regional Center (MORC), special education bus (SERVI-CAR), Social Security Income (SSI), and Special Summer Camp (SCAMP).

Jennifer's insatiable love of music, born of her drumstick duet with Frank, flourished at SCAMP, the day camp she began attending when she was five years old. SCAMP was designed to help special needs children thrive during the summer months, bridging their school semesters with the therapeutic benefits of singing, arts and crafts, cookouts, boating, and fishing. The founders knew that idle time can have a devastating effect on whatever a special education student has achieved in a school year. They also knew, because they were parents of disabled children themselves, the loneliness of months spent sitting at home, and that even those confined to the most challenging bodies and minds are capable of pleasure – the scent of waves, the crackle of a campfire, the taste of a hotdog.

The SCAMPers, who had every kind of disability imaginable, began each morning with a sing-along that was designed to get their enthusiasm flowing. Ranging from kindergarten age to adulthood, they waddled, wobbled, wheeled, and wormed their way into a local gymnasium, where the SCAMP pianist set the day's tone with the first of several rousing tunes.

For Jennifer, the sing-along was an earthbound heaven. There she could unleash her unabashed passion, her voice syncing with those of her friends, her joy doing likewise.

In one old SCAMP photo, Jennifer's hands and those of her peers can be seen tickling the air, performing an accompaniment in sign language for the benefit of those SCAMPers who couldn't speak or hear. Fingers form shapes and move toward faces, rapt in the pleasure that only music can bring – *Head and Shoulders, Knees and Toes; Little Bunny Foo-foo; Row, Row, Row Your Boat; Sunshine On My Shoulders.*

Since those early days, Jennifer's eclectic tastes have tended to run in long stretches, during which she'd play a favorite song over and over and over for weeks and months, sometimes years, before mysteriously giving up on it and turning her attention to another. She obsessively wound through Cookie Monster's *C is for Cookie* before moving on to Dire Straights' *The Walk of Life,* before switching to Wynonna Judd's *Tell Me Why* and then, finally, Celine Dion's mournful but lovely *My Heart Will Go On* – a song she first heard at the movie theater when James

Cameron's *Titanic* was released in 1997, and which nearly two decades later still sends her into squeals of delight whenever she hears it, never mind that she might be in an elevator, a doctor's office, or a grocery store.

One day, a rumor made its way through the neighborhood surrounding the school where SCAMP was held. The singer John Denver was in town to play a concert and, unlike anyone before or since, he had initiated a pick-up ball game on the school's diamond. After the game, he planned to stop by SCAMP for an impromptu sing. Some counselor or another must have let on that there was magic happening nearby.

I glided from home to the school on top of the rumor, like a bobber pulled along on a fishing line, and wended my way through a gathering crowd to find Jennifer in the midst of it. I snuggled her on my lap and assumed a position where we could see. We, like everyone in the audience, were filled with that peculiar energy that comes with the anticipation of seeing someone famous. We wore faces of expectancy, while across the room a mop-haired blonde in a baseball cap threaded his way through the SCAMPers and to the forefront, where he settled in a chair. The SCAMP pianist, with an unprecedented vigor, struck up the chords to Denver's hit song *Sunshine On My Shoulders* and he began to sing, as if the cue were meant for him.

Only a few short moments elapsed before the SCAMPers joined in, their throaty, awkward voices slurring the words "sunshine on my shoulders makes me happy". The SCAMPers' faces and bodies were twisted and turned as if seen in a funhouse mirror, but their hands and fingers danced like a gathering of fairies as they signed the words in the air. I could hear Jennifer's tiny voice just to the front of me, and feel the vibrations of her delight as she bobbed against my chest.

Denver, clearly astonished and deeply moved, attempted to follow the SCAMPers' lead. He waltzed his fingers tentatively up before his face in an attempt to join them, but his voice faltered then faded then stopped. Silenced by the enormity of what he was witnessing, he placed his hands in his lap and allowed himself to melt into the experience that was his song come to life. When a misshapen teenaged SCAMPer shyly ventured over to embrace him, he reciprocated without so much as a flinch of distaste or revulsion or fear.

I clutched Jennifer tightly, memorizing Denver's dignity, and said nothing more than "Thank you" when I introduced him to her and shook his hand. I looked him in the eyes and just this once my heart soared. For the first time, I didn't owe the world an apology.

Satisfaction Trumps Absurdity

In the 1980s, when Jennifer was about seven years old, I joined the staff of *The Clarkston News* as a reporter. Taking this job, I believed, would result in the fulfillment of my life-long dream – the publication of my writing. As a ten-year-old, I had stood in the living room, looked into my mother's eyes, and announced that I was going to be a writer when I grew up. The notion came to me out of the air. I had no idea how I would accomplish this and wasn't even much of a reader then. Nevertheless, this was my resolve, and between the ages of ten and twenty I wrote poetry and short stories and a few freelance business articles.

My first day at the paper, I sat down at my wooden desk, surrounded by the barn-wood walls, the ephemera of the newspaper that decorated them, and the other employees, and beamed over the good fortune that not only would I be a work-ing writer, I would have the perk of writing for the community I lived in, and which I loved. I felt this was more than a lucky happenstance, it was serendipity. Experience, both professional and personal, could build upon itself.

I quickly fell in step with small town journalism and its idiosyncrasies, and the job became my portal into the world, a way to stay involved, to stimulate and expand my life when I was otherwise consumed by Jennifer's increasing needs.

During my first year or so at the paper, hardly a week passed when we did not visit a doctor's office or hospital. She required speech, occupational, and physical therapy several times a week, and at five her left knee cap had begun dislocating in a way that puzzled orthopedic surgeons. Her knee became inflamed and swollen, and I shuffled her among specialists trying to find help. I was determined Jennifer would have the best life possible, and that she would sustain that hard-won ability to walk, and I pursued physicians and treatments tirelessly.

At the same time, I endeavored to achieve a normal childhood for Holly, driving her to baton and piano lessons, participating as a school volunteer, taking her to Sunday school, hosting sleepovers with her friends, orchestrating beach time. Like so many other women of the era, I believed that a woman can be and have it all – housewife, mother, professional. I was challenged but also fulfilled and interested in life. I got Holly and Jennifer off to school in the morning and faced my day with expectation.

A few months into the job, I was assigned to cover a township board meeting at which a resident was fighting to keep group homes out of our community. The man was on a mission – a cruel one it seemed to me – and came to the meeting to spew a host of reasons why group homes in neighborhoods were a bad idea. They were a new concept at the time, and some people were afraid of the unknown and how it might affect their property values.

Because I was present as a reporter, I couldn't voice any opposition to what he was saying. So I sat quietly and took notes for the news article I would have to write in the morning. Deeply moved by the situation and this man's obvious prejudices, I also wrote a column, my first, expressing my concern over where Jennifer would live when Don and I died.

The inevitability of death is a real worry for parents with handicapped children. The disabilities themselves present enough obstacles, it doesn't help to have people who aren't facing these problems complicating things.

I wrote in a rush of passion, the power of the piece touching a nerve I hadn't anticipated. Readers who had disabled family members wrote letters to me or phoned to speak of their own circumstances. I was surprised how many were in situations comparable to ours, some with children more disabled than Jennifer, who were quietly living out their challenges away from the public eye. I unexpectedly found myself giving them a voice. What was to become my "calling" – and ultimately the impetus for this book – began to click into place and to flourish at the newspaper's tiny office on Main Street.

If I often wrote about Jennifer, that doesn't mean I spared the rest of us. I affectionately called Don "The Perfectionist" in an effort to keep his name private while paying tribute to his taciturn nature, and I poked gentle fun at the light-hearted side of our life – what I called, to his dismay, our "adventures". I wrote about his response when I smoked up the house burning his mother's ancient feather pillow. I wrote about his response when I flooded the basement by way of the upstairs kitchen. I wrote about him chasing me around that same kitchen while I tested my new rollerblades, and I wrote about my wishing we'd been childhood playmates. I wrote about taking Holly to rock concerts. I wrote about cooking disasters and bad hairdos and cat foibles, and, when he came along later, our son Christian's non-stop questions.

By its very nature – evening meetings, afternoon deadlines, appointment interviews, articles and columns that could be written from home - the job provided me with flexible hours, making it easy to stay employed during Jennifer's most turbulent years, at least for a while. I often banged out copy at night, while alone in the office, my back to the big window that overlooked downtown Clarkston, or at my bedroom desk, while Don and the kids relaxed in the living room.

In my years of reporting for *The Clarkston News*, I traipsed around our coverage area – the City of the Village of Clarkston and Independence and Springfield townships. I wrote the hard news – politicians making demands, government problems, community development trends, school situations, crimes investigated by the sheriff's department, and fires extinguished by the fire department. I covered the occasional murder or robbery or rape or domestic abuse case, one tornado that devastated a mobile home park, and the advent of a lone bear who wandered into a neighborhood from northern Michigan. I sat and listened, sometimes trying not to cry, while men and women told me of their sons or daughters gone to war, or the deaths of their loved ones in car accidents. I met an untold number of people and went into their businesses and homes and churches and schools, learning about their hobbies, their treasures, their opinions of the world, and their dramas, all of which interested me.

If other reporters wanted to ascend the journalism ladder at the country's big daily newspapers, I loved talking to the unassuming, quirky folks who made the Clarkston area tick. Among them were an artist who created jewelry out of lobster shells, the owner of a herd of miniature horses, a family that kept a tiger caged in their yard, a fiddle prodigy, a saw player, the owners of a worm farm, a veterinarian performing a C-section on an iguana, a Christmas tree farmer who was missing a finger, an astronomer, a ribbon twirler, and, on a day when we were desperate for news, a woman in the character of Little Bo Peep, as she prepared to participate in the Detroit Thanksgiving Day Parade. I listened to her intently as if I were interviewing Princess Diana, and I took notes, trying not to laugh at the absurdity of it, while Bo Peep shared her ambitions.

My job also put me in frequent contact with Dr. O'Neill. He was busy trying to bring an urgent care center to Clarkston, going through the hoops and hurdles of architectural design and state licensing, and presenting his project to the planning commission or township board for zoning approval. I would sit in the journalists' section of the room and watch while he ambled in, his longish white hair and beard wild. He was sometimes in his lab coat, and sometimes had galoshes on his feet. His larger-than-life presence would overtake the room as he parked himself in a chair and tried not to doze while the township officials droned on about other developments.

Sometimes I called on him when an article had a medical twist and needed a professional's voice, and sometimes I found him at the center of a feature article, such as when I wrote about his historic farm as part of a series I was doing on the automobile magnate Henry Ford, who had owned the O'Neill homestead in the 1930s.

In a memory that I love to return to, I went to the county courthouse once to cover a trial. I don't recall the specifics of it, but Dr. O'Neill was sitting on the bench in front of me, waiting to give expert testimony. I remember that as the proceedings began and an attorney stepped to the podium before the judge, the doctor turned to me and whispered under his breath, referring to the lawyer's oddly-shaped bald head, "Nine'll get you ten that guy was a breech birth."

I had to suppress my laughter. I liked that Dr. O'Neill was comfortable enough to crack jokes in the courtroom, and that he'd singled me out for this one.

The Goings-On Inside Jennifer

It was the fourth night of what seemed like an interminable illness. Exhausted from almost no sleep, I was little more than a zombie as I crawled onto Jennifer's bed, beside her. She was a five-year-old ember, glowing deep red and giving off heat. I didn't need to touch her to feel it. The heat wafted towards me and settled on my skin like smoke from a bonfire. Indeed, her temperature warmed the room.

Jennifer's hair was glued in sweaty clumps across her eyebrows. I put my hand out and gently brushed these clumps away to expose her face. She slept through this gesture, trembling as if the bed was vibrating her, and I leaned across on one elbow to put my cheek against her forehead. I then lifted her tiny undershirt at the hem and put my cheek to her belly. I let it linger there, like a woman who had laid her ear onto a drum. Jennifer's stomach growled its displeasure at me, but I had discerned what I needed to know. Her fever was very high. Experience told my cheek it was more than 102, or even 103 degrees. Hers was the fever of the very sick.

I slid away from her and found the thermometer on the

night table, where I had left it late in the afternoon. I had used it so many times that week that its three flat sides had become familiar. The thermometer fit between my thumb and fingertips, as naturally as one of my pens. I held it to the light filtering in from the hallway and squinted to see the mercury trapped in the glass, a thread of red beside the notch that indicated 103, her temperature of only a few hours prior. I pinched the thermometer and began to shake it down. Shake. Shake.

I could hear my arm as it rushed the air. I shook it and looked until I saw that the thread had descended to where there were no numbers, down by the silver ball tip.

I lifted Jennifer's limp arm and gently placed the thermometer into her armpit, lowering her arm and closing her skin around it, tight. I compressed this spot, skin against skin, so that not even a whisper could penetrate and cause a fluctuation in the numbers. I waited for the timer I had set to register the passing of seven long minutes, counting the seconds away in my head – *One hippopotamus, two hippopotamus, three ...*

This fever frightened me. Her tremors frightened me. I was afraid they were going to gather their collective energy and throw her into a seizure. I was afraid that her fragile brain was going to cook inside her skull.

Jennifer's fever had soared to 105 degrees. I set the thermometer back on the table and ran to fill the tub with water, as tepid as that of a spring pond on a Michigan May day. While the bathtub filled, I hurried to the kitchen and pulled a purple Popsicle from the freezer. I snatched its wrapper away and hurried back to Jennifer, lifting her from her almost impenetrable sleep. She moaned at me and tried to focus as I handed her the soothing Popsicle and swooped her to the bathroom. She trembled as I placed her into the water and let her steep there, like meat in a marinade. Slobbery purple coated her lips and ran down, striping her belly and casting faint color into the water. I could hear her crunching the ice, slurping, shivering.

She looked at me like I was the one with the mental problem. A Popsicle here, in the bathtub? Now?

But it was my hope that this combination of inner and outer cooling would bring her temperature down. This was a day when I allowed Jennifer all the Popsicles she could hold, to keep her hydrated, to keep her ornery urinary tract functioning.

Surely my change in behavior confused her. Hadn't I scolded her endlessly for her multitude of kitchen raids, for the times she pocketed slabs of cheese? The times she stole yogurts?

It wasn't all that long ago that she had raided the freezer while I was out mowing the lawn and I'd had to reprimand her for overindulging. I could imagine her in this game of hers – alone in the house, seizing her opportunity, standing on her tiptoes, pressing her hands and head into the freezer, riffling through this cavern until she came up with her prize, a box of Popsicles, her eyes as delighted as those of a winning game show contestant.

I had come in from my hour-long chore to find her seated before the television, an entire box of Popsicle sticks aligned on the carpeting in a semi-circle around her, like splayed peacock feathers, the shadows of red and orange and green and purple barely visible in their wood.

"Jennifer," I droned, both frustrated and amused, "you're going to make yourself sick!"

Deep inside Jennifer, her left kidney struggled to do the work of two. Bacteria, little gangsters that they were, had infiltrated her through her urethra, traveled up it as if they were ascending the walls of a gorge. Once they reached her bladder, they raced for the kidney – and into the shriveled stump that pretended to be a kidney on her right side. They festered and stewed there, and multiplied, until Jennifer's system gathered itself in a counter assault and tried to drive them out by using its own fire.

This was not her first kidney infection, but I'd never seen Jennifer this sick, or her temperature this high.

I lay beside her whenever she ran a fever, scared that I would miss some surge and that it would claim her when I was unaware. And so I lay there this night, all night. Mine was the tenuous, jittery sleep of a guard dog. I relied entirely on my nerve endings. In the quiet of our household, I could hear her labored breathing, as if she could force the disease out through her nostrils. I could hear my own heartbeat.

On the morning of the fifth day, I phoned Dr. O'Neill for the third or fourth time that week, and he ordered her into the hospital, as much, I knew, for my sake as for hers. Her temperature, though, had finally dropped to 102.

A few short months later, Dr. Dare – so aptly named, this curmudgeon of an orthopedic surgeon – walked away from his own patient to peer into Jennifer's crib and say, "Does she always cry like that?" His shoulders were perpetually hunched, as if he had done nothing in his lifetime but stoop over operating tables and repair broken bones. His eyes were a steel blue and his head was covered in white silk – thick and alluring as angel hair.

These features were misleading. They disguised a man invested in his grouchiness. I could not help but be interested in him, as if he were a thespian instead, using his wiles to challenge and entice me. British, he filled the hospital room with his Anthony Hopkins voice and matching presence.

"Not always," I said. I couldn't believe the absurdity of his question. What little girl wouldn't cry with a big slice in her belly? I was conscious of the way Dr. Dare's and my energy bounced off of us, and then off of Jennifer. We were Mother of Comfort, Man of Science, Child of Tragedy.

Jennifer, now five, had been crying for hours. With a rubber drainage tube erupting from her bladder through her gut and out into the hospital's air, she had been in the throes of excruciating pain for three days. The tube wiggled its head at us, like a fat earthworm surfacing in the ground, each time Jennifer let out a yelp.

I reached in to pet her hair and coo, "It's okay, honey" – as if she could possibly believe this. My mind circled the moment when the orderlies wheeled her back from the operating room and she caught a glimpse of me from the hangover of her anesthesia and tried to fly into my arms, her freshly sutured abdomen squeezing in the effort, a surge of pain overtaking her and throwing her back onto the cot.

I couldn't believe that Jennifer's knee was failing now, before she could recover from her anti-reflux surgery, undertaken to stop the backwash of urine from her bladder into her kidney. Her urologist, Dr. Graham, had only just snipped out the stubby, sick ureter that sought its end in the phantom kidney. And I had only just asked, "If there's no kidney to receive it, where does the ureter go?"

"It just ends in her stomach, perhaps in her intestines," he had replied and shrugged, as if this were a matter of common sense.

I could see how this had gotten the better of her health. How the stump had withered and finally rotted, on foreign terrain. She'd had so many infections I'd lost count, and she'd taken so many antibiotics that she'd grown resistant to those few that didn't cause allergic reactions. We'd finally reached the point where there was nothing left to do but operate.

After her surgery, the nurses pumped Jennifer full of Demerol to alleviate pain so that when she was not crying she drowsed, fitfully. We held onto each other throughout the ordeal, and then her left kneecap began to pop in and out. Pop. Tick. I noticed it for the first time during one of those moments when I stood looking at her in her hospital bed. One of those moments such as I was having with Dr. Dare.

Each pop attracted my attention and diverted my gaze when I took her onto my lap. First the kneecap was atop her knee joint, like it was supposed to be. And then, with her foot pointed outward, it slid over to the outside of her leg, as if toes and cap were joined by a rubber band. She bent her knee slightly and, Pop! With a sound like that of a teenager's cracked knuckle, the kneecap resounded as it slid back into place.

In and out, in and out, the kneecap went through more repetitions than a child circling through a screen door during summertime.

Several months after her bladder surgery, I followed an invitation Dr. Dare had made while standing beside her bed, and I took Jennifer to see him in his office. The first of four orthopedic surgeons we would ultimately consult, he contended that sometime in the distant future soft tissue surgery could be performed to put the kneecap back into place. There was no hurry. A dislocated kneecap, while visually disturbing, is not a serious condition, he noted. A person doesn't need a kneecap to survive. And he flexed her legs up and down, side to side as if to prove this. He considered her and thought about what such a surgery might entail. Looking then, directly at me, he appeared to read my mind, to see there, beyond my puzzled face, the churning of thoughts – a young mother counting her family's resources, pondering her extended obligations, mapping the steps in the quest that might normalize, if not her child, at least this appendage.

"You can't make a silk purse out of a sow's ear," he finally announced, penetrating me with his eyes. It was this line, so indelicate, so offensive, so terribly, terribly true, that stayed with me.

Over time, Jennifer's leg became the axis around which our world spun, and increasingly our world spun out of control. The kneecap, as if in a game of one-upmanship, began to pop more frequently, and with greater ease. Jennifer played at orchestrating its movements. She sat on the couch, watching *Sesame Street* and, in time with "C is for Cookie" or "Put Down the Duckie" swung her lower leg with the rhythm of a metronome – pop-tick, pop-tick, time passed until finally the kneecap wearied of the game and came to a resigned rest on the outside of her thigh.

I could see the kneecap there, like a seashell beneath her skin. Sometimes I manipulated it the way I'd seen the doctors do, putting the tips of all four fingers and thumb around it in a circle position. I felt how hard it was, pushed it slightly to see if it would shift. This tickled Jennifer, who laughed and jerked the leg away.

I also noticed that Jennifer's leg had begun to angle into a new position. The leg, at the knee, became a wide, sideways V, with the lower part, the tibia and fibula, pushed backwards into what is called a subluxation. The tibia and fibula also rotated outward from the knee. The joint itself was puffed up soft, like a marshmallow, and inflamed.

Jennifer finally gave up, too. Finding herself to be a victim of frequent falls, unable to trust that her leg would support her, and stymied by pain, she quit walking. For two or three years, during which I scouted out specialists, she had to be carried everywhere, a task that most often fell to Don. He picked her up in his arms – her shoulders draped over his left arm, her legs over the right – and he hefted her to and from the car, through stores, to church services, and to family gatherings.

Fearing that she would never walk again, I undertook a quest unlike any I had undertaken before, ushering Jennifer through a revolving door of doctors. There was nothing I wouldn't do, and there was no place I wouldn't go, to get her on her feet again.

As a result, over that period of two or three years until she was about eight, orthopedic surgeons from far and wide scratched their heads over Jennifer's knee, not knowing what to make of it. They measured and bent it and held meetings in which they said, "I've never seen anything like this before."

Unlike Dr. Dare, who had recommended a waiting game, they put it in casts and braces, and took it out of them. X-ray technicians captured the leg on film and those films were carted around the country to medical conferences. At times, physical therapists put the leg through hell. Records were kept. Dialogues erupted. Nurses considered the leg in wonder.

Finally, a casual acquaintance named Rebecca – a friend of a friend who gossiped about us – came into the newsroom to tell me about Dr. Stan, a visionary who specialized in replacing the joints of adults with rheumatoid arthritis.

At Rebecca's urging, he agreed to examine Jennifer, even though she was a child and well out of the range of his specialty. She said he did not want us to make an appointment, rather, we were to show up at his office around lunchtime on a Thursday and trust, which we, in our desperation, did.

It turned out he had successfully operated on eleven similar legs – mostly those of Down Syndrome children. He had invented an operation that would have Jennifer walking again. Internationally famous for his innovation and skill, the great irony was that he maintained his practice less than one hour from our home.

By the time Jennifer saw Dr. Stan, I had become the maternal equivalent of a bumper on a car jack. I had been ratcheted up and up and up from Dr. Dare's comment that she might need soft tissue surgery someday to her third orthopedic surgeon Dr. Line's final exasperating recommendation to fuse her leg at the knee. Dr. Number Two, whose name eludes me, had placed Jennifer in a leg brace, a recommendation that Dr. Line disagreed with.

Sure, Dr. Line had said, in so many words, *if her leg is fused it will stick straight out like a poker for the rest of her life, but at least she'll be able to walk.*

Oh, and it will stop growing.

If they fused the knee soon it would stay age eight while the other leg went through puberty and became a woman's leg, or something akin to one. Didn't I want to go home and think about it?

I went home and envisioned the leg going about its business. Not fitting between the seats of the school bus or car, never pedaling again, the sole of its foot touching the wall opposite the toilet when Jennifer went to the bathroom. I pictured myself yelling, "Coming about!" Like a sailor handling a sailboat boom, every time I helped swing her into a restaurant chair.

We abandoned Dr. Line's practice and I hung on every word Dr. Stan uttered during our initial visit. "The surgery is risky. There are no guarantees. The leg might become paralyzed as a result, or infected, or not heal, or she might need subsequent surgeries. Or, Jennifer might even end up losing the leg altogether."

"Without surgery," he continued, holding her foot and peering up at me, "she might never walk again."

Here it was, her only chance, struggling like a fly in a spider's web, and I had to bear down on her like a black widow. I took this information home to Don and presented it to him. My face was, I'm sure, a scary wasteland. He was frozen in my gaze. I felt as if my head was made of mud and my eyes were a pair of stones.

Given the gravity of the situation, the decision seemed already made for us, and so we agreed to the surgery fairly quickly. We must do what we could to keep Jennifer walking – we must follow the thread of hope.

Months after the four-hour operation, when I was compiling her medical records and surgery information to send to Dr. Rubinstein, of the Rubinstein and Taybi duo, to share with other similarly stricken RTS families, I read the surgical report Dr. Stan had dictated. I read how he had sliced that long, lazy S into her flesh, down from the hip and across and below the left knee onto her upper shin. How he, looking within her, had located and identified parts of the leg's anatomy – except for the vastus medialis, which was altogether missing. How he had delicately slithered his scalpel along major blood vessels and nerves and cut a 4 x 3 inch piece of meat from her thigh – known as the fascia lata – then put it in a dish of saline for later use as human filler.

Spotting her knee cap, then, he isolated it and went about the intricate, painstaking work of putting it in its rightful place, along with the quadriceps muscle mass that had permanently slipped with it to the outside of her leg.

When he came to Don and me in the recovery room, he explained it in words like this – you must think of Jennifer's leg as being like an archer's bow. The bones, bent at exactly the spot where the archer's hand might grab the frame, have grown at one pace. The muscles, taut as the string with which the arrow is notched, have grown at another, causing the complicated deformity that forces her tibia and fibula to slide back from the femur, turns them ninety degrees, then folds the knee joint V-like, sideways upon itself.

Even now, as I re-read Dr. Stan's report to gather the facts over a decade later, I feel the same curious but compelling shiver I felt when I first read it so many years ago. Wanting to hide my eyes but unable to look away, I go through the pages, and follow Dr. Stan as he ventures forth on hallowed ground.

Much Ado Over A Toe

Several weeks after her knee surgery, I placed Jennifer on the examining table in Dr. O'Neill's office and waited for him to whoosh in. He always whooshed, never just walked. His step was weighty and hurried and filled with purpose, as if something irresistible pulled at him from the future.

I knew how things would go before he arrived. He would throw a distracted greeting at me and ask what kind of problem plagued Jennifer, but he wouldn't wait for me to tell him. Instead, he would run his eyes over her, from top to bottom, peer into her nose and throat and ears, listen to her chest and back with his stethoscope, and run his fingers down her spine, checking for scoliosis. He would inspect the fresh scar on her leg then notice that her socks and shoes were off, and would realize that one of her two big toes was the problem. The infected toe throbbed at Dr. O'Neill, like a baked potato letting off steam.

Jennifer sat rounded, waiting, a wedge of baby fat pinched between her chest and thighs. Her stubby legs shot out in front of her, and they rotated out from her hips so that her feet rested like the heads of Number 9 golf clubs laid on a fairway. Her feet were thicker than average, making them box-like in shape. If I painted her toenails red, they looked like ruby-studded jewelry boxes. When we played *This Little Piggy Went to Market* on her right foot's Siamese twin great toe, I said, beginning with it, "This little piggy went to market, and this little piggy tagged along."

Jennifer did not understand that she shouldn't have a tag-along piggy, but she laughed because I laughed. I laughed at my cleverness, and because my touch tickled her, which in turn tickled me.

The great toe on Jennifer's left foot is not doubled like the one on the right, but it is unusually big. Like its right foot counterpart, it probably has twice the number of bones on the inside, mirror image bones. On the outside the toe looks like a bat, and it has one huge toenail that grows under the edges of the skin. On this day, the skin was inflamed, purple, and oozing with an infection that could travel to the site of her leg surgery.

Dr. O'Neill whooshed in, as expected, wearing a black and red striped, long-sleeved shirt that reminded me of a sailor's. It fit his figure snugly, showing solid shoulders above a paunch. Dr. O'Neill planted a kiss on Jennifer's hair and worked his way to the toe. "Oh," he said, "that looks bad. If the infection gets in her bone you'll have a nightmare."

Dr. O'Neill was not much on bedside manner, and I knew this, but still the word *nightmare* was a little unsettling. I recalled the ordeal of the knee surgery and Jennifer's subsequent excruciating pain, and told him, "We've had all the nightmares we need, thanks."

Dr. O'Neill said he could take care of the toe in his office and began to work quickly. He always worked quickly when children were involved. He didn't bother to explain things to them, or to soothe their tears. He simply got busy with the task at hand, trying to bring a quick end to everybody's misery – the weeping child's, the worrying parent's, his own. He'd once told me that polio during childhood had left him so that his back hurts when he stoops over children all day.

Dr. O'Neill slid a lighted headband with magnified eye-pieces over his head so he'd be able to see clearly as he worked on the toe. He put rubber gloves on his hands and sat at the end of the examining table, his back to us, Jennifer's left foot clutched in one hand, her calf pinned between his arm and ribs.

"Have her lie down," he said to me, and I urged Jennifer onto her back, pressing my shoulders, chest and elbows over her stomach and chest, immobilizing her so she could neither see what he was doing nor jerk her foot away. Jennifer's expression was full of innocence and trust.

Dr. O'Neill is a Republican who likes to talk about politics, and he made an effort to deflect my concern with conversation. He shouted something about President Reagan over his shoulder, over my shoulder, and I turned to look at him, his comment lost in the air.

I could see that he had wound a thick rubber band around Jennifer's toe and that it had cut off the circulation so that the toe would not hemorrhage when he made his incision.

I grimaced and my heart attempted to bolt. The toe was standing up. The doctor had a large syringe full of anesthesia in his hand and as he pushed it deep into Jennifer's skin, beside the nail, I felt her flinch and heard her gasp as he worked it first this way, and then that. Her back arched against the table, her chest pushed me, her head was a boulder weighing her shoulders down.

I pushed myself more fully across her. "Don't move. Don't move," I said into her ear. My lips brushed against the warm velvet of it. Her breath riffled my hair. I was a reluctant oppressor, and I hated the way I used my size and strength against my own child. I hated the way I was forced to side with the doctor, the way I must necessarily compound Jennifer's distress. I could not help but wonder if this experience would forever change the way she perceived me, if I would, in her eyes, become Mother with a hint of Monster.

I tucked my face into the nape of Jennifer's neck and she squirmed against me. We were so close that I could feel the vibrations of her squeals in my own throat. My cheek and forehead, wet with a commingling of our sweat and tears, slid against her skin, while Jennifer's left arm made its way to freedom. I felt the shift between us, the sudden release of energy and space as it escaped. The arm went up and then fell across my back.

I raised myself, knowing that I must find it and force it down again. I could not allow the arm to rage against this indecency. I came up to search and noticed that Jennifer's light brown hair was open around her face. She focused on me. In those few moments, my cheeks and eyes became swollen and puffed and red.

I could vacantly feel Dr. O'Neill's rapid movements against my back, trying to hurry through his task, but other than that I was scarcely aware of him. From the periphery of my vision, I saw Jennifer's arm rise, the elbow bend, the fist on the end come close to my head. I anticipated a swing, a blow. Jennifer had only this one hand to use. I had the other pinned still, and I grappled and watched and bobbed as if this flying one were a catfish flailing on a line.

A tuft of white flashed from between Jennifer's curled fingers – a forgotten tissue, wadded now, scrunched down into a tight ball, a victim of Jennifer's fear. She brought it between our faces and released the bulk of the tissue into the air, deftly retaining one edge between her finger and thumb. Jennifer surprised me when she did not put the tissue to her own eyes, but instead laid it against mine. Jennifer dabbed at me, blotted first one side and then the other.

"Mama," she said, with a touch to my left eye. Hers was

a two-stroke rhythm. She touched the right. "Why are you crying?"

In A Community Of Bones

By the end of Jennifer's first year of post-surgical physical therapy, my abdomen was hugely distended with the infant who would become her brother, Christian, who would soon be born normally. It went before me as I entered the hospital's physical therapy room, bobbing up and down as if I had a helium balloon beneath my blouse. The lesser balloons that were my breasts bounced, too. I walked on spongy feet, the ankles of which overflowed my shoes, and I had a spongy nose. My nose had grown so big that I had to look around it when I read. It taunted me over the newspaper. "See me here? I'm yours. See how pink I am? See how bulbous?"

I was one swollen, pent-up mama. I retained so much water that I joked I might be called Lake Mama. Even Great Lake Mama, here in the Great Lakes state of Michigan. I looked forward to the burst that would expel this child, and my equally huge anxiety over what might emerge.

What a long pregnancy this was. I went about my life thinking, *I hope, I hope, I hope, I hope ... this child will not have Rubinstein-Taybi Syndrome.*

Jennifer, now ten, spotted me from across the gymnasium-sized room. She broke the strain in it with the only thing about her that was unfettered, her unabashed adoration of me.

"Mama, you look so beautiful!" she called, as the faces of others fell upon me, laughing. I tried to shrink from the embarrassment of this pregnancy.

Jennifer, I could see, had been bound to the wooden stretching table by her physical therapist, Linda, while I was on my walk around the first floor. Linda had banished me, not wanting my distraction, not wanting me to endure Jennifer's plaintive cries, not wanting me to shout comfort while she tormented my child in the name of healing. Jennifer was on her back and a series of wide electric chair-type straps criss-crossed her chest and arms, her hips, her legs at the knees, her ankles. They flattened her and held her in place, though she was squirming and resisting mightily. Her clothes were in a wrinkled bunch.

Linda depressed a foot pedal and activated the motorized table, bringing it up from prone to standing position, tilting Jennifer, reluctantly, onto her bare foot and leg. Linda's fingers leveled the foot full against a board, a step at the bottom edge, and like a dog that can hear but not argue back, the foot was told to prepare itself. Linda waved her hand over the foot and cautioned it, "Stay."

The whole contraption forced Jennifer's twisted, scarred, tight left leg into a more proper, straight alignment. Linda was slowly easing responsibility back onto this leg. Physical therapy was a long, tedious process – three mornings a week of alarm and crying. But Jennifer … was … going … to … walk … again … someday, so help me, God.

She did not want to stand up. It flat-out hurt. It hurt on the inside, where the muscles and sinew and bone and blood vessels had been re-routed. It hurt along the length of the twelve-inch scar that meandered its way from her hip to below her knee.

The scar, keloid and thick as rope, looked like red piping sewn onto the seam of Jennifer's skin. I remembered when it didn't used to be there, how her leg had been creamy and smooth. I remembered how I had gently touched this leg one last time before surgery. I had touched it to imbed its innocence and beauty in my mind. I had touched it for luck.

It was so hard to motivate Jennifer. She didn't want to sit in the therapy whirlpool, she was afraid of it. She didn't want to practice her exercises at all. Long explanations were lost in her simple mind. Coaxing didn't do any good. Bribes didn't work much better. She contorted her face in distress. She mouthed what appeared to be spells, witchy curses that Linda and I couldn't hear. She'd had enough of, "But, Jennifer, you want to walk! Sure you do."

No. She wanted to race wheelchairs with the amputees, and to play catch with the huge rubber balls, like the stroke patients did. She wanted to get the hell out of there.

While I was gone walking, Linda glued little electrodes to Jennifer's left thigh and jolted her with a current designed to stun and relax her tight muscles. The muscles were so rigid, so shrunk, so long out of use, that Jennifer had no control over them. She couldn't straighten that leg and run in terror if someone lit a fire to her backside. She couldn't straighten that leg and run in anticipation if Cookie Monster himself lured her with a Snickerdoodle. Posed against one another, her good leg and her bad leg formed a lazy Figure 4 that would last forever if Linda couldn't get her on her feet again. The surgery, with its months' of excruciating post-operative pain, would have been for nothing.

"This will tickle," I know Linda lied while delivering the jolts. I'd heard her lie before.

Despite its yellow walls and cream-colored curtains and cartoon murals, the therapy room was every bit a torture chamber – a room of ropes and pulleys and hooks and spikes and hot oils and steel machines, a room of clangs and whirrs and buzzes and squelched screams. We could hear the old lady beyond the curtain begging, "No, don't. Please!" We could hear the deep-throated pleas for mercy that came from a cubicle just beyond her. "Stop. Let me alone."

Jennifer wriggled her left hand down through the straps and rubbed the top of her thigh with her square fingertips. Linda put her hands over the straps and looked at the floor and counted under her breath. Jennifer would have to stand like this for twenty long minutes.

A deep sadness filled me the day Linda finally threw her hands in the air and told me that there was nothing more she could do for Jennifer's leg. It had been whirl-pooled, electro-shocked, massaged, manipulated, stretched, and exercised for over a period of four years and, while her leg was *almost* straight, it wasn't quite straight. The residual tightness behind her knee, called a "flexion contracture" had outsmarted everyone. At age fourteen, she still couldn't walk.

During this period, Dr. Stan had taken her back into the hospital a series of times, and under anesthesia tried to help by progressively relaxing her leg enough to put it in a walking cast, hoping that a few months of uninterrupted torture would have an effect. They didn't. When the casts were removed, each one progressively more straight than the one that went before it, Jennifer's leg engaged its memory and contracted to the shape of a hex key. The pull of her determined hamstrings overrode her capacity to use her thigh muscles.

Dr. Stan told me he could not understand this. The leg cooperated when she was asleep. He'd held it in his own two hands. Joining Linda and me in exasperation, he believed the problem was Jennifer's willpower and agreed when Linda finally suggested that I take Jennifer to a Shriners Hospital, where the doctors dealt exclusively with children who had orthopedic problems. Maybe they'd have some ideas, Linda had said.

And so, on a blustery fall day Jennifer and I drove to Detroit to join other hopeful families for the 6 AM ride to Pennsylvania on a Shriners bus. The wonderful Shriners organization had promised free transportation, free meals, free medical care, free hospitalization, free surgery and, if need be, free physical therapy and a brace for Jennifer, the same as it had for every other patient. A jovial, middle-aged Shriner, the bus driver, and his wife welcomed us aboard and we settled ourselves on a seat for what would turn out to be the first of many six-hour rides to the land of state-of-the-art miracles. After she had yet another surgery to release the flexion contracture, we would make follow-up trips over a period of three or four years on beautiful summer days and in snow blizzards, dining on Shriners sandwiches and playing Shriners games.

With our first step into the clinic lobby of the Shriners Hospital, I realized that we had arrived at a place unlike any we'd ever been to before. I felt as Dorothy must have felt when she woke up in Munchkinland. We were blinded by a shock of primary colors – slides and pull toys and playhouses populated by children of every configuration imaginable, and in some cases unimaginable. There were children in casts using their arms to pedal modified beds, wheelchairs, or bikes. There were children with artificial limbs scampering around the Shriners clown. There was even one boy, a blue-eyed dwarf, who raced his peers on legs that were being stretched in devices that looked like Ferris wheels attached to his calves and shins with pins. Over a period of months, these devices would, incredibly, lengthen his legs to a more normal length.

Jennifer reacted to this setting as she might have reacted were she to visit the *Sesame Street* set, and once she was checked in she joined the other children in play until we were ushered to an examining room, where a doctor who looked like trumpeter Al Hirt confirmed the flexion contracture diagnosis and told me that it could be corrected with an operation that would involve loosening – that is cutting – her hamstrings behind the knee.

As the morning passed, she was attended by professionals of every nature – surgeons, orthopedic residents, nurses, physical therapists, men who built braces – and their attention was so thorough to both her and me that I soon realized we had made the right decision. I could smell the delicious scents of lunch emanating from down the hall, and from a distant window I could see the playground the patients used when able. There was a homeyness to this hospital, and despite the frightening sound of the operation, *tendon release surgery*, I found myself growing at ease.

Thus began the final steps in our journey to getting Jennifer back on her feet.

On the day before her surgery, I was given a small room with a bed and a dresser, reserved for out-of-town parents, on the second floor of the hospital, just above the girls' ward, where I would stay while Jennifer underwent and recovered from her operation. Don remained at home with Holly and Christian for what was anticipated to be a one-week stay. I wasn't happy about seeing Jennifer through surgery by myself, but the task was made easier by the Shriners Hospital ambience, promise, and fabulous staff.

The ward Jennifer was on contained beds for ten girls, most of which were occupied. In some cases, mothers sat beside their daughters – interestingly, no fathers were in sight. Having other mothers to talk with during the hours of waiting for tests and surgeries was wonderful. We comforted one another as much as we comforted our children. It felt like we were all part of a strange, exclusive club.

In many cases, the girls were alone. They ranged in age from two years or so to the mid-teens and came from all over the world. Among them were a mother and daughter from Poland, whom I befriended, and adorable Amish children dressed in modest garb that was not able to conceal their freckles or their charm.

Jessica, the ten-year-old girl in the bed next to Jennifer's who would be having extensive surgery on her spine to correct a spina bifida defect, having listened to Jennifer talk non-stop for a while after her admission, wryly asked me if Jennifer talked in her sleep. Her intelligence and friendliness offered me a comfort I did not expect, one she was too young to recognize. I laughed at her wit, and thought that this girl would be good company for Jennifer, and maybe even a guardian when I was asleep upstairs. It was reassuring to know that someone with common sense – someone who could summon the nurses if need be – would be resting nearby in my absence. Summoning nurses was a task that was beyond Jennifer, or so I thought.

Across from Jennifer was a twelve-year-old girl with a boyish name, Billie Jo, who was awaiting the delivery of a prosthetic arm and leg. She was engaged in a conversation with the teen next to her, who, wearing the face of middle school evil, had just asked, "Billie Jo, are you afraid to die?"

Billie Jo, who had obviously faced death in the form of an unspeakable accident, said she was not afraid to die. But she said this in a whisper while looking into her lap.

At the far end of their row the Polish mother skimmed through her Polish to English dictionary in an attempt to converse with the nurses. Her brown-black eyes, set in a beautiful face, were wide and round. Her young daughter, who had cerebral palsy, was scheduled to have surgery soon. I wondered what it must be like to entrust your child to strangers from the other side of the world, who speak a different language from your own. Their situation, their aloneness, their vulnerability, put Jennifer's and mine into a fresh perspective.

Periodically everyone, mothers and daughters alike, looked up to smile and stare when the Brad Pitt look-a-like physical therapist entered the room.

Later in the day, Jennifer and these girls would join boys from the boys' ward and a teacher for school lessons and then arts and crafts or games. At night they would be feted with ice cream sundaes. The ambiance was so generally pleasant that I would have forgotten we were in a hospital if my mind were not dwelling on the operation I knew was to come.

No matter how many surgeries Jennifer underwent – by this time, there had been six spread among her eyes, her bladder and her leg – I always worried. What if there were anesthesia problems? What if the operation didn't work? What if, this time, she came out of recovery, focused her resentment on me, and said, "I hate you!"

On the morning of her surgery, I waited with Jennifer in the pre-op room where nurses prepped her with a tranquilizer and washed her leg, flushing antiseptic soap and warm water up and down her skin. Jennifer was only vaguely aware of what was about to take place and I was working to not emote concern. I tilted my head serenely, petted her hair, and uttered reassurances. Once she was taken away I ventured back to the ward to await her, but got just a few steps before my pent up tears came.

Only a couple of days passed after the operation before the doctors realized that a staph infection had set into Jennifer's incision, posing a serious new problem. If the infection took hold she could become gravely ill. They replaced her cast with a clean one and carved a square opening – a window – into the back of it so that they could observe the incision's healing while giving her antibiotics. I was informed that she would have to stay in the hospital for another month of treatment, meaning that I would be torn between staying with her and going home to be with Don and Holly and, in particular, Christian, who by then was four years old. I knew that Don and Holly, who now was eighteen, could take care of themselves, but I was worried about the effect my prolonged absence might have on my son, who was old enough to miss me, but not old enough to grasp what was happening, or to understand my need to be away.

I decided to stay with Jennifer a week and then go home

for a visit, ultimately bringing Holly and Christian back to Shriners with me. We stayed with Jessica's mother in their nearby home and attempted to create a sort of mini-life, going to the zoo and the beach when we weren't with Jennifer – while Don maintained his work schedule, a practice that, by now, had become a source of frustration for me. His faithfulness as a wage earner notwithstanding, I had long since lost track of how many times I'd sat alone with Jennifer in a hospital or medical setting, aching for his companionship, oftentimes making important decisions by myself, the weight of which began to accrue over the years.

"Children need their mothers," Don would say, arguing that he couldn't take off from work every time Jennifer was hospitalized, while I argued that they need their fathers too. I suspected he held his conviction because in his own childhood it had been his mother, and not his father, who had been the meaningful presence.

There was a dim part of me that understood Don's predicament – Jennifer had been hospitalized so many times due to illness or surgery no employer would agree to that many absences from an employee.

Ours was an impossible conundrum. This difference in our needs would present one of the biggest challenges in our marriage, and I would sometimes wonder if this was a worry in the families of other disabled children – even as I knew from reading and through some of my friends that divorce and abandonment are commonplace in such families. My anger would go underground and fester the way anger does, and I would always be glad that Jennifer could not understand this, lest she somehow feel responsible for my disenchantment.

During the few days when I was in Michigan, I fretted and called Jennifer to make sure she was doing okay and she screeched her love back to me over the phone lines during brief conversations.

I learned later from the charge nurse that while I was home worrying and arguing with Don about whether or not he would return with me, our daughter was alternately helping shuffle papers at the nurses' desk, joking with the staff, and cruising the hospital in a wheelchair, and that, one night, the Brad Pitt look-a-like had taken her on a "date" to a Red Lobster restaurant and the zoo. It was a Shriners policy to take the patients on outings once they had passed the one-month hospitalization mark. After a six-week stay in the hospital, the staph infection now gone, the operation successful, Jennifer arrived home only to produce photographs that proved she'd had a great time.

I learned an important lesson from this. Contrary to what I thought, Jennifer could get along perfectly well without Don or me. It was a lesson we would resurrect when the time came to move her from our home as an adult. Jennifer, it was becoming apparent, had harnessed the key to happiness, and she was far more independent than we were giving her credit for.

A few weeks after her release from the hospital a card arrived in the mail, addressed to me. It was written by that same charge nurse, a stunning reminder about the importance of perspective. My angst had been the nurses' joy. It said:

"Dear Mrs. Walker,

I've debated about writing this note; ethically speaking nurses, particularly supervisors, are not to show partiality for one patient over another. But I couldn't let these wonderful past couple of weeks go by without telling you how much we appreciated Jennifer's charming company. She has provided us with a refreshing dose of innocence and joy that has been sorely needed. Our days have been so much brighter with her here."

Out Holcomb Road

When I wanted solitude, time to reflect, a chance to get away from responsibility, to think, to dream and imagine, I took a contemplative drive out Holcomb Road, past Dr. O'Neill's house. I'd been there on a few occasions, both professionally and personally – once to cover a congressman's political rally for the newspaper, once when Dr. O'Neill stitched a gash in Jennifer's head, and once when I went to interview him and his wife about the history of their farm, as part of a series of features I was writing about Henry Ford's connection to Clarkston. Ford had used the property for what was called an "experimental farm," raising soybeans there and training Ford officials in the use of the then new Ford tractor.

Named for one of Clarkston's early residents, Holcomb Road begins at a busy intersection, and it runs from there for miles into what is left of the area's countryside. A cemetery, a lake, and a park border its southern-most end, just at the point where Clarkston's historical homes begin their march through time. At its most remote northern end, where there are still some gentleman farms, Holcomb Road is a two-lane, dirt road lined with pine, maple, oak, elm, birch, scrub trees, and wild flowers that flank the occasional house or barn. Birds swoop and chirp from the arms of the trees. Lilacs fill the air with their pleasing scent.

Dr. O'Neill's three-hundred acre farm is located not too far past I-75, maybe a mile or so of stretch and rise over the freeway from Clarkston's downtown. He once told me that when they were building I-75 in the early 1960s, the construction drove rattlesnakes out of the woods and into the open of his yard. His daughter jump-started his heart when she went after one with a spray can she found in the barn.

In one of the memories for which I am most grateful, I see myself as I stroll contentedly in that yard with Dr. O'Neill, eating strawberries with him in his garden, discussing a wide range of topics, watching the pine trees that rim the farm as they fade from green to silhouette with the setting of the sun.

That evening, I had been to his office after hours to interview him for a newspaper article about the death of one of his patients, a sweet little boy who made the news because his heart and lungs were the first ever to be transplanted into another child.

For some reason that he never explained, Dr. O'Neill often came to his office without a car. One of his loved ones would come get him when he was ready to go home for the night. I'd seen this happen.

This time, I was handy and Dr. O'Neill asked me to give him a ride. I was surprised, but I did this happily, glad for the chance to have time with him and a more casual conversation. Dr. O'Neill frequently gave me ideas for the newspaper. He was a fount of interesting information and fascinating stories regarding people, politics, culture, the state of medicine, and his boyhood on a farm in the Dakotas. As I drove, we exchanged glances each time a tire hit a pothole. It was hard to avoid them on this dirt road, and we both recognized how silly he looked bouncing up and down. When we reached his farm, he walked me around his yard, across the grass, past a grazing horse, past the huge white barn that would soon burn to the ground in an accidental fire, and then into the garden he was so proud of. Along the way, he pointed out facts about this or that. The garden, Dr. O'Neill told me, was his "psychiatrist." When he needed relaxation or to organize his thoughts, it was the garden he turned to.

I could see why. It was large, inviting, all shades of comforting green, its straight rows filled with a variety of vegetables, then the thigh-high strawberry bushes, lush with fruit, set in an adjacent patch. When we reached it, he planted his shoes into the earth and picked some - I was not presumptuous enough to pick any on my own – and he shared them with me. The experience only served to deepen my affection for him. I watched as he shoved a berry into his mouth, the red coloring his lips, then extended one to me. They were sweet as candy, the temperature of the warm air, and filled with juice. Sometimes he picked faster than I could eat, and I put the spare berries into my pockets, where they leaked, sticking my clothes to my flesh.

Whenever I drove out Holcomb Road, I slowed my car in front of the O'Neills', reflected on that garden stroll, and thought, somewhat longingly, about the lives they must live there, the day-to-day goings on of running a farm, the family banter, the affection. From all appearances, Dr. O'Neill and his wife had a happy marriage with six beautiful children. I was sure they were close to one another and enjoyed the merriment of a lively, full home. I would learn soon enough that even the generous and gifted Dr. O'Neill was not immune to heartbreak.

My trips down Holcomb did not end at the O'Neill farm of course. I continued its length until it dead-ended at another road, made a right turn and followed that one until it met another, and so on until I'd explored a country maze. My drives would last an hour or so, and on them I would take in the life that surrounded me. If I was lucky that meant seeing a deer, usually a doe, sometimes several, which for some reason thrilled me every time. Evidence of the beautiful. Grace and elegance, pure and true, bounding through fields or darting across the road.

At one point during our walk, as we faced the setting sun, Dr. O'Neill grumbled mildly about the deer that sometimes feasted in his garden. I listened. But in that moment, I was happy for them, even envious of their freedom, their access to this lovely land, this lovely man.

There was always a plenitude of birds on my drives – robins, sparrows, blue jays, crows. In the fall, V's of Canadian Geese flew above the trees and honked. When I passed homes, I saw that various families had dogs, cats, horses or cows, and occasionally llamas or alpacas in their yards. And of course there was the abundance of trees, which I loved. They shaded the road and stroked the sky with their limbs, or reached them down to brush my car as I passed by.

Sometimes a stand of trees opened itself so that I could see behind it. There were old clapboard farmhouses with American flags on poles in their yards, others were newer, with brick and aluminum siding and basketball hoops.

When I passed these places I imagined the people who lived in them. Pictured little boys running around bare-chested on the lawn, or girls playing dolls in their sun dresses. I thought the parents must be conversing agreeably over coffee, or doing chores. If it was November, I was sure they were celebrating Thanksgiving with their relatives, around big tables resplendent with food and drink. At Christmastime, I pondered the decorated trees standing in their living room windows, bright with multi-colored lights and ornaments and the promise of festivities.

My jobs in the emergency room and at the newspaper had taught me of course that the lives of others were not necessarily easier than mine, and oftentimes they were more difficult – a parent running frantically to the front desk after receiving an emergency call about a terrible injury to her child, families grieving in a huddle after losing all they owned to a house fire. Nevertheless, part of the pleasure of my drives came from my fantasy that the families along Holcomb Road and beyond were happy-go-lucky and joyous – that such lives surely existed somewhere near.

I made these drives maybe once or twice a month for several years, watching the inevitable consequence of development as the acreage of aging residents was given over to subdivisions. Even the O'Neills, as Dr. and Mrs. O'Neill became older and their children grew up, allowed much of their land to be developed. They kept their house and its immediate several acres, and to my dismay made a pond of what was once the garden. It is now clearly visible from the newly-paved road, sparkling as pretty as champagne in a glass. In the back of the property, a plaque explains the farm's history, and across from that there are the scattered, multi-million dollar homes of people wealthy enough to buy them. Many of the trees – over 80,000 evergreens planted by the O'Neills – were saved by the developer, so that the houses are in the woods, and the neighborhood has the feel of a glorified campsite, at least to me.

Like Graduated Ripples

I learned of the death of Dr. and Mrs. O'Neill's adult son while at his office for Christian's six-week, well-baby check-up. When a nurse escorted us into an examining room to be seen by Dr. O'Neill's associate, I noticed how wan and drawn her face was, the color of coffee with too much cream. Then I became aware of the silence that permeated the building. Expecting to show Christian off, I hadn't noticed it at first.

"What's wrong?" I asked her.

"Dr. O'Neill's son is dead," she said. She stated this softly but bluntly. She concentrated on my face, the weight of her sadness transferring to me. I felt reasonably sure she wasn't telling this to every patient's mother, but that she was sharing the news with me because she knew I had a professional relationship with him through the newspaper, my having covered the government certifying process for his urgent care center a few months back. I had attended that meeting in another city with Dr. O'Neill, this same nurse, and the now deceased son.

I could hardly take it in. It was the most unjust news I could imagine, that this man who had saved so many children, comforted so many parents, had now lost a child of his own.

"Oh, no," I said to the nurse, my voice falling off. I held Christian, feeling his baby warmth against my chest.

On the day of the funeral, I found myself sitting in a church with hundreds of people, a soloist singing a mournful but beautiful hymn from the balcony behind us, then standing along with many of these same people at the graveside service, which took place in a tiny cemetery that adjoined the home for the aging Jesuit priests Dr. O'Neill cared for when he made house calls. Above us, an almost white sun shone out from a blue sky. This brightness was the one thing we could all be thankful for, for it made our collective ache just bearable.

To hone in even closer, the sun shined full on Dr. O'Neill, highlighted his crystal blue eyes and the smile, now forced. His body showed its age that day. He looked as fragile and delicate as the wand of a willow.

I watched as he tangled his arms before his chest and pressed his feet beneath him in a way that was reminiscent of how he stood when we ate strawberries in his garden. The gestures seemed to shore him up somehow. For the sake of everyone present, Dr. O'Neill had to be strong.

We all loved him, and did not want to stare at him, though it was difficult not to. Our eyes, meant to be downcast, were inevitably drawn to him. We awaited his cue, knowing that if he cried we would all cry. And if we all cried ... well, the Jesuits' grounds would get a soaking. It must have been nearly impossible for him, but Dr. O'Neill did not cry.

I'm still not sure how I managed to get so physically close to him, given the size of the crowd and the fact that I was not a member of his family, or even of his close cadre of friends. It was not intentional on my part. I simply jostled into place, like a penny that rolled and bumped off other loose change.

In truth, I was not even sure I should be in attendance.

I had followed the invitation of others who knew Dr. O'Neill better than I. They said, "It's okay, Carolyn. Come along," and asked me to join them in their car. One of them, a lovely old man, a collector of antique medical artifacts whom I had featured in the newspaper, even rested a compassionate hand on my shoulder.

Dr. O'Neill was there, to the right and just forward from me, looking across the cemetery at the pine trees, which might have been distantly related to those that framed his farm.

His sad wife, dressed in a simple dress, was speaking in whispers with her closest friend, who, having also lost a child, understood her shock and pain. The remaining O'Neill children talked to their friends.

Farther out, like graduated ripples on the surface of a pond, were rings of civic leaders, fellow parishioners, teachers, other doctors, friends and relatives of the O'Neills, and schoolmates of their son.

I stood silently, respectfully, knowing that if I were to lean into the person closest to me I would mumble, "What was God thinking?" And that person would say, "Yes, I was wondering that too." And then he would lean into the person next to him and become my echo. And on it would go, from person to person, ring to ring, until my question became the crowd's – "Why does this man have to suffer in this way?"

Dr. O'Neill turned to me, unexpectedly. My fingers were knit together, prayer-like, in front of my stomach, doing double duty. They were supplicant in the absence of words. They held my insides, inside. I looked at the mahogany casket. Like Dr. O'Neill, its polished finish glinted under the sunlight. It had golden handles, and a layer of deep red roses was splayed across its top. Poles stretched beneath it, in a perfect rectangle, holding it aloft over a fresh hole. The earth in that hole, beneath Clarkston, was a rich dark brown.

"How's your little one?" Dr. O'Neill asked, surprising me, and he reached an arm around to embrace me. I felt it fall across my shoulder and tug. I heard the bristles of his beard, the only sound in the cemetery, as it scratched into my hair.

If he squeezes even slightly too hard, I thought, I will shatter into a thousand jagged shards. I relaxed into his arms and buried my face, fleetingly, against his chest. I wiped my tears on his shirt, hoping that he didn't realize this.

"He's fine," I said, coming up to breathe. I thought Dr. O'Neill was asking me about Christian. I was amazed that he would ask me about my son while burying his own.

There was a pause. Dr. O'Neill had forgotten that I now had a son. He was lost in the years that predated Christian. "She means a great deal to me," he said, and he looked me in the eyes, and bobbed his head in a way that meant, *Yes, this is true.* It was then I knew that Dr. O'Neill had been asking about Jennifer, a fixture in my shadow.

Hearts Come At A Premium

For years I kept my letters from Dr. Jack Rubinstein in an oversized, flag-colored envelope that became as ragged from use as *Old Glory*. Our correspondence, which took place once or twice a year, was essentially simple, the two of us sharing concurrent curiosities – me wanting to know as much as possible about the cause and effect of what I called "Jennifer's Syndrome", turning to him like he was some kind of diviner, and he, engaged in research, wanting to know as much as possible about the ins-and-outs of Jennifer's development.

After the 1960s, Dr. Rubinstein had taken his studies out of the mental hospital realm and into society, and he had endeavored to learn about as many RTS children as possible, comparing how the syndrome affected each one – their hearts, their intelligence, their extremities, their health. At the time of Jennifer's birth there were only a few hundred RTS children known to be alive in the world, so each new patient provided him with fresh insight.

When I first contacted him, he sent me a long questionnaire asking, among other things, how and when she had been diagnosed, as well as how old she had been when she passed her various developmental milestones. I answered Dr. Rubinstein's questions from my kitchen table, running down a checklist of her symptoms, and hustled the document into the mail as if it were burning my fingers.

While I sat writing, I pictured Dr. Rubinstein ensconced in a small white office in Ohio, wearing a suit and tie and glasses, poring over a handful of letters sent to him by mothers like me, collating us like an accountant collates his figures.

I was forthcoming in my letters, talking about Jennifer's body functions with a feigned clinical detachment, one that I appropriated while working in the ER, while Dr. Rubinstein was kind and informative, writing with a tone that was both professional and fatherly.

"Nice to hear from you. How is Jennifer doing?" he would write. "Anything changed or new?"

"Basically fine," I would respond, though I progressively noted her complications. They've discovered a twenty percent hearing loss. I've started taking her to a speech therapist. The doctors can hear a heart murmur. She has impossible consti-pation. They think she has a blood-clotting defect. She almost died from thrush in her lungs. She has funny bumps on the backs of her teeth. She has gastro-esophageal reflux. She's being checked for melanoma. What is Spina Bifida Occulta? Jennifer has gained a lot of weight. Is it likely she'll have normal peri-ods? Is Jennifer going to develop breasts? What would happen if Jennifer got pregnant?

During Jennifer's teenage years, another mother who had been corresponding with Dr. Rubinstein helped him organize a conference in Ohio, where parents and children would be allowed to meet one another, share stories and advice, and confer with specialists in the fields of pediatrics, gastroenterol-ogy, cardiology, orthopedics, neurology, audiology, endocrinol-ogy, plastic surgery, and dentistry.

Up until this time, I had met only one other individual with RTS. Given its rarity, I had been living with the belief that there must be no other people with the syndrome in our immediate, or even extended, radius.

Jennifer and I met the gregarious Billy on an elevator during one of Jennifer's visits at Children's Hospital. His face and thumbs, of course, gave him away, and I quickly exchanged phone numbers with his mother, who seemed equally surprised by the encounter as I was.

We were both grateful to discover someone who shared our circumstance, and she and I maintained phone contact for years, until the evening she called to tell me that Billy was in need of a heart transplant, and that he had been rejected from the waiting list. He was by this time twenty-one years old, and her husband had abandoned them a few years prior.

Hearts come at a premium, she told me, and it is required that recipients have the capacity to care for themselves and maintain the strict medical protocol that is assigned them. I can still feel the way love flooded her despair, which fell over me like a slow, cold rain that has nowhere to go but down.

Once we got to the conference in an expansive downtown hotel in Cincinnati, I found it infinitely bizarre to be sur-rounded by people who wore Jennifer's face. It was as if we had walked into a giant house of mirrors. They were everywhere, reflecting one another – in the dining room, in the restrooms, in the halls, in the corners where their parents, overwhelmed as Don and I, fed them from baby bottles or changed their diapers and tried to quiet their concerns. The children, in their sameness, were like mannequins come to life, each individual a variation on one human theme. Each head small, each nose beaked, each smile endearing but a little off.

The conference came much later in Jennifer's life than I might have wished when she was a teenager – too late to help solve or even inform solutions to most of her problems, but timely enough that we might at least learn what to expect of menstruation – that ominous, still in-the-offing body function that I hoped would present her last growing up challenge.

And, it was timely enough that we might share our walk and talk and school stories with newer parents who were trying to come to terms with what had transformed their families and redirected their dreams.

With Christian and Jennifer in tow and Holly off at college, Don and I climbed the stairway from the hotel lobby to the mezzanine to fill out papers and make our presence at the conference known. This seemed like such a silly thing to do since Jennifer's face gave our purpose away. Jennifer and I fell into line with other mothers and children, Don and Christian loitering in the background, and as we stood there it occurred to me that we mothers had our similarities too, expectant yet somewhat resigned demeanors. We affirmed one another with nods or quiet hellos, not as the strangers we were, but as conspirators on a common mission. Yes, that is what we were – Seekers of Truth. Alongside us stood the siblings and the bewildered fathers, hands in pockets, Adam's apples bobbing.

There was a girl in front of Jennifer and me who spontaneously turned to speak. Unlike many of the children present, she could talk. I was immediately charmed by her. She looked and acted so much like Jennifer that she was both delightful and unnerving to me. More than just her face, which was Jennifer's carbon copy, she exuded my daughter's personality from a similar form, a mini-pudge of happiness and enthusiasm and interest. I felt my maternal instincts swell, as if I might pull her into my arms and embrace her as my own. I did not do this, of course. Instead, I tightened my grasp on Jennifer's hand and had this fleeting thought – if Jennifer were to die, I could find myself in a crowd sometime, looking into a face that was hers, but also not hers. I ran some fingers through my hair, not so much to realign it as to help push this thought from my mind.

I was brought out of this thinking when the girl introduced herself to Jennifer.

"Hi, I'm Nancy," she began. She stood at the same height as Jennifer, 4'7", and looked her squarely in the eyes. She extended her hands before her waist to take Jennifer's. She offered them freely, and as Jennifer reached back both sets of thumbs stood out like those of hitchhikers while their stubby fingers intertwined. I watched while the clear, unmistakable look of revelation washed over my daughter's face. She was frozen in this instant of recognition.

In a flash, I understood for the first time that Jennifer understood, even though she could not articulate what was happening. She didn't bother to try. Delighted to find that she had been duplicated, she embraced Nancy as her long lost twin. She squealed a "Hi, how ya doin'?" that was so loud and so authentic it went straight through me, but it didn't seem to faze Nancy. They took each other in fully and appreciatively. They bounced a little and then Nancy turned to me. She had to aim her head up to find my eyes. Her expression beseeched me.

"Does she have the same syndrome as me?" she asked.

I was taken aback by her question. Stunned that she knew she had a syndrome, much less the ability to discuss it. I told Nancy "Yes," as the line began to shift forward. Beyond her, her mother nodded knowingly, and with acceptance. She was giving me permission to have this conversation.

Nancy's question and the exchange of glances between her mother and me were completely lost to Jennifer, whom I wasn't sure had an awareness of her syndrome. She always seemed gloriously oblivious to it. And it had never occurred to me to bring the subject to her attention.

It was not until day two that we met Dr. Rubinstein seated in the hotel lobby, which was alive with a flurry of activity. Parents milled about and children played in groups, while others could be heard crying in the background. Buoyed by Jennifer's accomplishments, juxtaposed against the arrested development of so many present, I walked over to him with the oomph of a stage mother, words of pride poised on my tongue. I introduced us, certain that he must be as thrilled to meet as I was. I was certain that he had been anticipating this very moment the same as I had. He looked up at us pleasantly enough, but with far less enchantment than I expected. I think he may have patted Jennifer on her head. I remember that he spoke to her and that she tipped down from my arms toward him, my palm encouraging her a little, her hair falling forward.

It never dawned on me that for Dr. Rubinstein, who had been fielding children non-stop like a juggler at a carnival, Jennifer's was just another face in the crowd.

Fie On Puberty

Dr. Rubinstein had told me in an early letter that there was no reason to suspect Jennifer's menstruation would be anything but normal. Still, puberty worried me because, well, it was puberty, that time in life when the predictable would become unpredictable, and when Jennifer would be at her most vulnerable. I had no idea what to expect from Jennifer's convoluted body, emotions or sexuality. I didn't know if she was going to grow great big breasts, or no breasts. I didn't know if she would bleed every month or never – or maybe once, just for good measure. I didn't know if she was going to have mood swings. And I didn't know if she was going to go boy-crazy. Among the worst of my fears was the possibility that someone would take advantage of her sexually. How could I send her out into the world and keep her safe at the same time?

As it happened, puberty announced itself during one of her checkups at Dr. Graham's office. We'd made trips to his office at regular intervals since she was five years old, the way other people go to church or on their vacations. Dr. Graham monitored the state of her urinary tract and prescribed maintenance antibiotics to keep it healthy, even after her anti-reflux surgery. While the surgery had cured her of kidney infections, she was still prone to bladder infections. Medicines like Sulfa or Macrodantin helped to keep them at bay, though periodically Jennifer would develop an allergy to whatever drug she was on, or it would lose its effectiveness due to extended use, and we'd have to start a cycle of new medication. The only way to ascertain the effectiveness of these drugs was for the doctor to analyze her urine regularly, and so I brought her once every three to six months to give a sample. Called a "clean catch specimen," this sample could only be taken after the germs were washed from Jennifer's skin.

On this day, Dr. Graham's nurse entered the examining room like a maid about to serve tea. She carried a stainless steel tray at waist level, upon which she had positioned a pitcher of clean water and a small bowl. A bleached white washcloth was folded over it, like a napkin. She set the tray on a countertop and stepped over to Jennifer, who was splayed out on an examination table, just as she had been splayed out scores of times before. Her knees were up and pointed at outward angles. Her feet were dwarfed in the silver stirrups, as if in rehearsal for her first pelvic exam. She had a grip on the edge of the table, her fingers denting its tan fabric the way they did my stomach fat when she had it pinched up in one of her tickling jokes.

I prodded one of her hands out of its grip and took it in mine, and comforted her while the nurse opened the folds of her skin and washed, rinsing the suds from between her legs with warm water that fell like a clear, soothing waterfall, from the pitcher. The nurse dabbed at her as if she were painting a watercolor, with an artist's sensitive touch.

Jennifer had her gaze focused on the ceiling, that part of it that was just beyond her, so that she had to extend her neck and roll her eyes high into their sockets. She accepted this treatment, grudgingly.

I wondered if she ever felt a sense of modesty or betrayal, if she had any awareness that she was exposing the most vulnerable part of herself to strangers, putting her femininity out there the same as she might a hand or foot. The closest she came to complaining was to offer a quiet moan.

The nurse and I talked in low tones as she washed. For me, there was something other-worldly about this experience, something intimate and raw, something neither wrong nor right.

The room was what might be described as a contrived white. Not the agreeable white of fresh snow or of cumulous cloud or even of the washcloth – it was infused by fluorescence on a rainy November day. As we overlooked Jennifer's crotch I felt as if I were hovering above a gorge, considering the one scraggly vine that I might clutch at if I fell.

A single brown hair appeared to be inching its way from her labia toward the light. I saw it, but I didn't want to see it. Or maybe I should say I didn't want to believe in it, the way I didn't want to believe in hell. I gestured with a forefinger but did not touch. The nurse watched as my finger hovered and wriggled like a worm on a hook.

"Do you suppose that's a pubic hair?" I asked her.

The nurse scrunched up her nose and lips, making fine lines where a mustache might be if she were a man. She examined the hair from a distance. She said, *Hmm*, and cocked her head. I sensed that she knew the answer but was afraid to state it, was afraid I might tip into the gorge if she said the wrong thing. I filled the moment's awkward silence with my fears.

"I dread puberty," I said. The nurse knew this without me having to tell her. If she were I, she would dread puberty too. I dreaded hair in Jennifer's armpits and hair on her legs. I dreaded a pimply face. I dreaded mood swings and training bras and, because of the fertility it would bring, her menstrual cycle. I dreaded all the implications this one hair carried.

I had no idea how to tell Jennifer about sex or pregnancy, whether knowledge would be armor that might protect her from men or boys who might try to take advantage of her, or whether it would fill her head with new and pleasant notions – with longings. So I opted to say nothing, choosing instead to deal with these matters if and when they presented themselves.

I looked the nurse in the eyes and made one more comment, my sarcasm betraying me, "You know, it figures this would be the one thing about Jennifer that is normal."

The nurse maintained a non-expressive face and patted Jennifer dry with a towel and we each took a hand to urge her back up the table and into a sitting position. Jennifer pushed the stirrups with her feet and allowed us to pull her upright. A big water stain lingered near the foot of the table, like a wet shadow.

As our visits to Dr. Graham measured out the pace of years, I watched while that single hair became one of many, her pubis darkening like a nest baking in the sun. Soon she sprouted breasts and I taught her awkward little hands with their jointless thumbs how to hook a bra in front of her and then circle the catch around to her back, so that the cups came forward and enveloped them.

Shadow Child

Over the years, I have become friends with other people who have disabled children, most of whom I met through the school system or SCAMP. Often we'd get into conversations about how our children were faring – that just seemed to be the track our dialogue inevitably took. We'd talk about their health issues, their doctors, their classroom conduct, their pastimes, their living arrangements, their body functions, their surgeries. Even when the topic was a tough one, we had a sense of humor about it.

"You don't get an instruction book when you get a kid like this," we'd joke. We'd allow a look of irony to pass across our faces, a mischievous fluttering of the eyelids accompanied by half smiles. We all understood what we meant, the make-it-up-as-you-go approach to parenting.

It is equally true in this kind of situation that you aren't issued instructions for how to balance the lives of your other children. The needs of the disabled child always lurk, calling for your attention, energy and discernment. Their needs inform the lives of every family member, sometimes in obvious ways, sometimes subtly.

You ask yourself – how can I set aside one-on-one time with my well children when someone less well constantly needs me? How much help do I ask of them, how much responsibility do I put on their shoulders? Is that passing on of responsibility really a teaching opportunity, or is it a form of escape? Are too many toys substituted for involvement, or to ease my conscience?

You do the best you can. You wing it.

Holly told me once that what bothered her most after Jennifer was born was that Don and I never explained her sister to her. We didn't take her aside and talk about the deformities and the developmental delays or Jennifer's odd look. Holly said she figured out her sister was handicapped when they were little, but didn't realize she was mentally retarded until she was about eight years old and someone at a gathering told her.

I remember, poignantly, how she came to me with her question. She arrived home, searched my face, and asked me if it was true. "Is Jennifer retarded?"

When I said, "Yes," it was like someone "pulled the rug out from under me," she observed later as an adult. As she spoke, I thought about how hard it had been for me to accept this truth about Jennifer, the how-can-this-be? The wishing-it-was-different. I wondered what Holly's understanding of mental retardation was at the time. It wasn't a word I'd ever defined for her. We'd not known anyone in a position to set an example.

I could only comment that an explanation about Jennifer never occurred to Don and me, although in hindsight, it seems like one should have come automatically. Shouldn't it have been our instinct to say to Holly, "This is how things are now, and these are the things that are going to change."?

Even now, in her early forties, Holly says she is always "waiting for the other shoe to drop." She has absorbed my nature in this regard – always on alert, always anticipating the next drama. Ours is a Pavlovian response. But rather than salivate like Pavlov's experimental dog awaiting food, we grow tense with anticipation of the next life-changing event.

"I get it, Mom," she said one day when we were talking about the way Don and I had succumbed to Jennifer's needs at her expense – or at least what felt like Holly's expense to me. She sounded a little exasperated, like I hadn't yet deduced that she was a grown woman with a good mind. Like I hadn't yet figured out she was capable of understanding. By this time, she was managing her own home, looking at the past through the lens of maturity. "I get it," she said. "It's okay." Her voice was insistent.

But it didn't feel okay to me. I thought it was her intellect and not her emotions talking. I recall my response to her bitterly, an impulsive comment that flowed from my guilt and regret, "Sometimes I feel like I can't remember your childhood."

Those might not have been my exact words. I might not have said, "sometimes." I might not have said, "I feel," but writing about it here, those three words, for me, soften the blow – the reality. They were, after all, a part of my intention. They showed that sometimes isn't always or everything, and that feelings aren't beliefs or knowledge.

I felt safe making myself vulnerable to Holly when I revealed my thoughts, although in second-guessing myself I think a mother who confesses to her child is more of a problem than the mother who made mistakes in the first place. She not only opens a can of worms, she shakes it up and lets them out afterwards.

Holly said she's never going to have children. The risk isn't worth it.

"Not out of my womb. No," was how she put it. She was adamant. And even though I understood and could sympathize with her reasoning, the comment stung. It meant she'd never make Don and me grandparents. It meant she'd never walk in anything that even remotely resembles my shoes – although I think she would say that just being a member of this family is a lesson, in and of itself. She would say she can do her mother-resembling perfectly well from where she's at in life, a happily married college professor.

When I made my confession, Holly said, "That's a shame" with what seemed to me like residual resentment. She asked, "Are Christian and I some kind of shadow children?"

That word "shadow" cut me straight in two. I told Holly in response, "I was afraid Jennifer was going to die," and even as I spoke those words I felt a return of the angst that dominated our life for so long. I felt the way I subconsciously prioritized my children's needs. For a time, there was silence on the phone, and then from Holly, "Sometimes I feel sad for us. I wish we could have a family epiphany."

It's not like I draw a complete blank about Holly's childhood. It's more like it moves through my mind with the clicks and stops of a reel-to-reel movie. I remember when she was a toddler and caught a garden snake and watched keenly as it wended its way through her fingers. Holly studied the snake while I, creeped out, ran around the yard yelling at Don to take it away from her. I probably looked as ridiculous as he later claimed, and Holly as innocent.

I remember her third birthday, how she cried when she saw the angel food cake formed as a dress around a doll figurine. I remember birthday five, too. We lived in Clarkston by that time. Overwhelmed, she fell to tears and ran to her room when the crowd of neighborhood children approached the front door for her party.

I remember sending her off for a week's stay at sixth-grade camp, and for two weeks in England when she was in high school, and then, when she was twenty-two, for seven months as a college exchange student in Mexico. Each trip was more extensive than the one that preceded it. Each goodbye tugged progressively harder at my heartstrings. I remember, too, dropping her off at the university dormitory for the first time. She hugged me, told me she loved me, turned her back, and walked away with her suitcase. She looked exactly like the eighteen-year-old me on that very same Western Michigan University campus some twenty years before – dark hair and eyes, slender build, a stride toward the future, an air of optimism. Holly doesn't know how hard it is to let a child go. Really, the birthing pains are nothing compared to that.

A star theme traveled through Holly's childhood, as if acknowledging that moment when I delivered Jennifer. One evening, while Don and Jennifer slept in our motel room, Holly and I sat on a wooden swing on the beach at Mackinaw City, where we always vacationed during Jennifer's younger years, and we talked as the stars winked their rhythm above that of the waves in Lake Huron. Mackinaw City was a fun, family-friendly, safe destination for Jennifer, and that was why we chose to go there every summer, rather than gallivant around the country or take a trip overseas. It was an area we all loved. But there was an overriding perk – roughly four or five hours from home, Mackinaw was far enough away to make us feel like we'd traveled, close enough that we could dash back to Dr. O'Neill if Jennifer became sick.

The waves licked the shoreline before Holly's and my feet. We kicked the swing into motion. In the distance, moonlight shone onto the water. I have no memory of what we discussed, instead, what I recall is the intimacy of our conversation. The warmth and sharing, the mother/daughter bonding.

Another night, I got the idea that Holly should see a shooting star. I think we had been talking about shooting stars, that maybe I'd been telling her about the one I saw fly in a long arc over my grandmother's house when I was little. I think I had been telling her about how tiny bits of serendipity occur in those quiet moments when we are least expectant.

I didn't want Holly to grow up having never seen a shooting star, and so we gathered up some blankets and pillows after dark had settled in. We lay down beside one another, just the two of us on our backs, on the raised deck, and we watched the sky for a couple of hours and talked about all kinds of things. Holly finally said she saw a shooting star, but I wondered if she said that to please me. Whatever she saw, it passed me by, and I was right there looking.

In The Wake Of A Bicycle

I saw Jennifer with a fresh clarity on a summer's day when she was a teenager of fifteen or sixteen. Poised on the brink of womanhood, she was all Jennifer – a surgically patched up version, to be sure, but nevertheless all Jennifer. The features of her Rubinstein-Taybi Syndrome, the beak nose, the sloping eyes, had long since faded into impishness and determination. For me, the act of looking at her had become like the act of looking into a slightly tarnished mirror. That which mattered lay just beyond the surface.

On this day, though, the reality that Jennifer's body was now fully developed was driven home in this singular image, which greeted me when I stepped out our front door – Jennifer wedged impossibly in her old, hand-me-down, low-slung tricycle.

Beneath the sun, in the distance of our driveway, she was a pear with a topping of caramel syrup – her long, silky hair cascading in a light brown shine over a plump face, rounds of breasts and spreading hips which had somehow emerged over the winter. She parked her bottom on the trike's pink seat, her breasts brushing the handlebars, and she sat patiently – too long in the body and legs to pull her feet up and pedal. She relaxed her shoulders and cocked her right arm onto the backrest, letting her left arm hang, and she poked her feet out sideways from the front wheel and sighed.

I knew she would sit without complaint and watch life pass, if need be. But I could not bear to watch her be thus contained, to endure this loss of freedom. The ability to pedal was too hard won. Her little circle of independence that was the cul-de-sac in front of our home was too precious to lose. I turned and went back into the house and placed a call to the bicycle shop, where I secretly ordered her an adult-sized, candy apple-red, three-wheeler with metal baskets at its sides.

Jennifer didn't understand what I meant when I said, "We're going to get you a new bike." On the day the order came in, she took my hand with considerable trepidation when we walked across the bicycle shop's parking lot. Maybe she thought I was deceiving her, making up a ruse to take her for a new dental or medical procedure. While I had never resorted to ruses, Jennifer had misgivings, born of an endless stream of appointments. Her experience with brick buildings, parking lots and sidewalks, like those in front of us, was narrowly defined.

We walked in a drizzle at Jennifer's ponderous pace, step-lurch, step-lurch, step-lurch. Her eyes widened as we drew closer to the store's picture window, in which, strung overhead like giant Christmas lights, hung a variety of red, yellow, and blue bicycles. I don't think she dared to imagine that this building might contain something glorious for her, something that was not going to poke or penetrate or attempt to fix her.

So it was that Jennifer entered the store, my reluctant follower. Caught by surprise in the ambiance of this wonderland, she took in the bicycles that surrounded us with a simple judgment – their beauty was astonishing. She relaxed and guessed that she could touch, but not sample, and she dropped my hand

and waddled up and down a few aisles.

I stood back to watch her, savoring her sudden, quiet pleasure. She stooped over the toddler training bikes and said, *Aw*. She patted the mountain bikes, the English racers, and even the exercise bikes, which might be pedaled for miles without moving so much as an inch forward. She rang the occasional bike bell, honked a rubber horn or two, and tugged at the tassels that hung from valentine colored bikes in the girls' section, but never, not once, did she say, "Can I have one?"

I watched her, sideways, while I whispered to the man behind the counter, "You have an adult three-wheeler here that I've ordered for my daughter." And he disappeared behind a wall only to re-emerge with a bike that made my eyes sting with its shine and promise.

"Jennifer," I called to her, "look at this." She was crouched beside a child's bike that was much too small for her, and she rotated her head up to look, her hands posed on her knees. The man and I might just as well have been standing there with a new pony.

"Wow!" she exclaimed, her face lighting up in the experience of epiphany. She formed this full sentence – "Do I get to keep it forever?"

The hum of business that pervaded the store came to an abrupt halt as patrons and employees paused to watch Jennifer eagerly stroke, then climb aboard her bike. She turned the handlebars to make the front wheel move. She pedaled up an aisle. She rode the bike through the shop's front door and over to our truck and watched with delight as the clerk and I hiked it up into the truck bed, damp with rain.

On the long drive home, Jennifer pivoted around to keep watch through the truck's back window. She gestured and squawked directions when her father and I lowered the bike onto the driveway. Grinning, she circled it around the cul-de-sac. She shook off the rain that now fell harder. She went with it into the sanctuary of the garage and sat contentedly on its seat when the rain became a downpour.

Over time, she took her beloved Cabbage Patch doll, Ethel, and her brother Christian for tours inside the baskets, eventually bicycling them the length of our street, and then the circumference of our neighborhood.

As her territory and confidence grew more expansive, so did the difficult realization that I needed to give her more freedom. Over the summers, I staggered the way I let her go. I pointed out *Stop* signs and then followed from behind. I walked slowly, at a distance, my eyes trailing her.

A few years after the purchase of the bike, after much pleasant riding, there came a day when Jennifer's heart could not abide the slow pace of time. With the promise of festivities roiling in the Clarkston air, I rummaged around inside a closet for my spring jacket while Don pulled her bicycle from the garage in our new, much more congested downtown neighbor-hood – a neighborhood with sidewalks and streets more like a city than the subdivision we had just moved from.

For reasons that mystified most people, including myself sometimes, Don and I, in lieu of the social life that had been taken from us after Jennifer's birth, had entertained ourselves over several television seasons with too many episodes of the *This Old House* show. We had also decided that we would further complicate our lives by restoring, just the two of us, a derelict, one-hundred-and-fifty-year-old house in the center of the City of the Village of Clarkston, which we would, in ten years' time, occupy. We were enamored of local history, and the history of this house in particular. It had been a birthing home during the 1920s – and we loved those occasions when we popped off boards in one room or another only to find old bottles or calendars hidden beneath them. We loved watching the house give up its treasures and come into its own.

After years of reconstruction that included ripping out floors, tearing off walls, re-plumbing, rewiring, re-roofing, adding on rooms, and much more, we had moved in. Holly was married and living on her own, Jennifer was in her early twenties, Christian was in grade school, and Don and I were aglow with the potential that new surroundings bring.

On this day, Jennifer had a focus, which she had been chatting up eagerly for a week. Her friends from SCAMP would be awaiting her in the nearby Depot Park for the annual SCAMP Walk-and-Roll fundraiser. A lifelong SCAMPer, her imagination knew this to be true, and only this. Don turned his back to shut the garage door, and Jennifer, now mounted on her bike, was gone – out the driveway, down the sidewalk, around the corner, into the street, toward the steep hill that flanked the park. She was gone at a breakneck ... no, at a free spirit's speed.

I can only imagine what happened next. She hit the hill with complete trust and anticipation, saw the gathering of friends just beyond it, felt the bike soar in one glorious moment of abandonment, pitched and rolled as she struggled to rein it in against the speed of its descent, then flew over the handlebars.

I picture her, round and fleshy, a human blimp cut loose from gravity, tumbling in slow motion with her hands outstretched before her, the whole of her hitting the asphalt with a solid smack and then sliding, her chin and face taking the brunt of the fall.

Don and I flew too when we realized she was gone. I took the footpath as fast as I could, circling around to the park, only to learn that no one knew where she was. Don came around a one-way side street in the car. We met in the park just in time to hear someone screech, "She's fallen! She's hurt!"

A stranger rushed toward me and extended a shaking, dirtied palm, a single tooth resting there, like an abandoned egg in a nest.

As if of a single ambition, we – family, friends and strangers – converged on Jennifer, found in a heap on the hill, her beloved bike a twisted wreckage of metal and rubber on its side, the wheels askew, her jaw broken, her face and shirt bloodied – a single oozing hole showing between her lips. I pulled her into my arms and glanced over her shoulder to the ground, just long enough to wonder how anyone had found a tooth amid the asphalt fragments and pebbles.

Don and I raced her home, and I quickly put the tooth in a baggy of milk to preserve it, as I'd learned to do while working in the emergency room. It sank, blending into this salving, liquid mother-of-pearl. I dabbed her face with a wet washcloth, wiping away streaks of blood, and tried to calm her. Jennifer cried like a baby. She bawled overtly, the *O* of her mouth shrinking and swelling, her voice an alarm releasing words without shape.

I called Dr. Spangler, our dentist, at home, and he stretched a soft, compassionate *Oh* into my receiver. He knew the enormity of this situation without seeing it – Jennifer, a high-risk patient, had nearly died while getting her wisdom teeth pulled only a few months before. Sight unseen, he knew the options for treating this injury would be limited.

"Bring her to the office," he told me. "I'll meet you there."

In the few seconds that remained before he disconnected, I heard him sigh and abandon the relaxation of his Sunday afternoon.

Dr. Spangler's office was as still as an empty chapel when we entered it, Jennifer's whimper the only sound. Don and I helped seat her in an examining chair, and we watched while Dr. Spangler, with the most gentle of gestures, spread her lips for a peek at the damage, delicately flexing her lower jaw on its hinges to assess its mobility. The jaw resisted. He took an X-ray that showed a fracture and some swelling on one side. He wiggled the loose tooth next to the hole. He numbed her and probed the inside of her mouth thoroughly, feeling his way along the ridges of her remaining teeth and gums. His fingertip was a spelunker in a tiny cave.

Satisfied that Jennifer's injuries were confined to the fracture and her two front teeth, Dr. Spangler fished the lost tooth out of the milk with a gloved hand and performed a root canal on it with precise, fine movements, while we all watched. It was easy to do a root canal on a tooth that he could hold in his hand. He fingered the tooth close to his face and focused as he worked, his lips pursed in concentration. Then, like a jeweler positioning a diamond in the most delicate of mountings, he nudged the tooth back into its hole, suturing it in place.

At this, Jennifer sat forward, tasted the tooth then threw her limbs before her in a desperate attempt to escape the chair.

"We'll have to wait and see if this takes," Dr. Spangler explained, resting a hand on her shoulder, pressing her back. "Usually, a tooth that has been knocked out and put back in is good for about three years, but I have seen them last as long as eleven."

I did some quick mental math to begin the countdown to when Jennifer might lose the tooth for good. I envisioned the slide that would take place, the way her teeth would converge on one another, like boxcars in a train wreck, a tooth deciding to fill in the gap. That tooth coaxing another along. Those left behind following the trend, until Jennifer had no upper teeth remaining. This could happen, I told myself, before she's thirty, or even before age twenty-five.

Dr. Spangler dared to summon another specter. "We need to think about what to do with her jaw." He worked his own jaw tensely. I could see the muscles twitching beneath the skin at his temples. Only six months prior to this accident he'd put her under anesthesia in a hospital to clean her teeth and fill cavities, while an oral surgeon removed her wisdom teeth. Theirs had been a partnership in preventative dentistry geared, ironically, at protecting her very delicate dental balance. Their best efforts had been followed by near disaster when she went into respiratory failure in the recovery room.

Despite the intervention of four medical specialists afterward, the cause of her emergency was never determined. What is known is that Jennifer awakened, took a breath and somehow sucked fluid from the pores of her lungs into their cavities, which filled like barrels under rain spouts.

Faced now with this fracture, we had a new and serious problem. Dr. Spangler recommended consultation with yet another specialist who would help us to decide whether or not more anesthesia and surgery to set Jennifer's jaw would be worth risking her life.

I cannot remember the name of the oral surgeon who helped make our decision a short while later. Nor can I recall his face. What comes to mind is the stark cleanliness of his office, all white and stainless steel with no personality. All empty rooms waiting for someone's trauma. He held Jennifer's cream and smoke colored X-ray up against a light for me to see, pointing out the fracture. It was there on an angle, down from a vacant, skeletal eye socket.

See it, appearing as if someone had taken a jigsaw to the bone?

He was a young man, a kind man, a brave man. Yes, he said, if we wanted he would try to set Jennifer's jaw. He would call upon his courage and dare the odds and place his bet that she could safely undergo anesthesia again. She had, after all, safely undergone it many times previously. "This one time might have been a fluke," he said.

He told me that if he were to set her jaw, Jennifer would have to endure having it wired shut for at least three months. She would have to do the impossible – go silent. She would have to eat through a straw. He said that if we didn't want her to undergo another operation, the jaw would heal in its now broken position, but that it would be functional – as long as she didn't challenge her already weak chewing skills with an edible variation of rubber. He pointed out that, cosmetically, the broken jaw didn't adversely affect her appearance.

I looked at Jennifer's face, at its natural deformities, and saw that, indeed, the accident had not made things noticeably worse in that regard. Her face had only shifted ever so slightly to the right. I looked, too, at her innocence and trust and I couldn't bear it.

This oral surgeon was a patient man. He told me I could go home and discuss the options with Don, that we could think and stew and brood and worry and come back when we had made a decision. I led Jennifer out of his office, my hand holding hers, and we went into the parking lot, into that afternoon's thunderstorm, with the weight of Jennifer's life straddling my back. I'm not sure whether I cowered because of the storm outside, or because of the one that raged within me, but cower I did. Finally, after bouncing the alternatives off Don like I was bouncing a basketball off a backboard, we decided the risk simply wasn't worth it.

Decades after Jennifer's fall from her bike, Dr. Spangler and I still reminisce when he cleans her teeth in his office, him yodeling a laughter-inducing accompaniment whenever Jennifer starts to whine. *It's Eklahoma. No it's Aklahoma. No it's Oklahoma,* he goes, mimicking Forgetful Jones from *Sesame Street.* Even with her mouth propped open and tears brewing in her eyes, Jennifer cannot stifle a chuckle when he does this.

Unlike medical procedures, which she has mostly taken in her stride, Jennifer still experiences dental procedures with the dread of a young child, rolling her head and crying or talking non-stop as a diversion tactic. Dr. Spangler uses his probe to poke at a little pus pocket, a gum pimple that has developed just above the rescued tooth. It is a natural side effect of her accident. It is a prognosticator. The state of the "boomp," as Jennifer and I call it, predicts the wellbeing of the tooth. As long as the bump is not inflamed, infected or draining, the tooth, Dr. Spangler tells me, is probably safe.

When Dr. Spangler talks about this tooth and Jennifer's near death, he pops his blue mask under his chin with his fingers and reflects, and my memories of Jennifer's respiratory failure after her oral surgery stack up on top of his.

On that fateful day, Dr. Spangler approached Don and me in the hospital's surgical waiting room, wearing an uncomfortable smile. His demeanor was one of tension, his eyes diverted down.

"Jennifer's having a little trouble breathing," he said.

A surge went through me. I had sat in too many waiting rooms, heard too many cautionary tales, and I challenged him, "How much is *a little*?" It struck me that a breathing problem should not coincide with dental extractions or anesthesia.

Jennifer had been through anesthesia at least twelve times, and surgeries far more complicated and longer than this one, and there had never been even a passing comment about her breathing. It also struck me that Dr. Spangler was not accustomed to delivering bad news. What was the worst news he might ever have to tell a parent? That a child's tooth has to come out? That a kid needs orthodontics?

"They're working with her now," he said. Hands clasped, he offered a shallow, monk-like bow. "Let me go check on her, and I'll be back to let you know when you can see her." Dr. Spangler pivoted professionally and vanished for a while. In point of fact, Jennifer was fighting for her life.

As Dr. Spangler explained it later, she breezed through the four-hour dental procedure, roused as expected in the recovery room, sat up, took a breath, and then keeled over in respiratory failure. It was a keen-eyed nurse who saw Jennifer's oxygen levels plummeting and summoned a physician, who re-established connection between the ventilator, used as a matter of routine in the operating room, and its still-in-her-throat hose, which saved her life.

"Fifteen minutes more and we would have lost her," Dr. Spangler said, a day later, when the drama was behind us. I watched his skin settle over his bones when he said this, as if he had raised his arms, donned a robe made of flesh and shaken himself into it. We were gathered in the hallway outside Jennifer's Intensive Care room. He had spent the night at the hospital and grown an overnight's worth of facial stubble.

Seeking the cause of the emergency, Dr. Spangler ultimately welcomed the opinions of a cardiologist, an infectious disease specialist, an anesthesiologist, and a pulmonary specialist but believed none of their four suspicions when they delivered them. They were at odds. It could have been an unknown heart defect. It could have been a secret infection. It could have been fluid overload from the IVs. It could have been that the airway tube was improperly placed, or that it kinked when she sat up.

Whatever had happened, Jennifer now lay flat on her back in the hospital bed, the respirator's blue hose coursing its way down her throat, the machine forcing air into her lungs with an even rhythm. Because of her circumstances, she could not talk, or even whimper. Her eyes darted back and forth, back and forth, her fingers flicked nervously, her pulse and blood pressure rates skyrocketed on the monitor, betraying her terror as the pulmonary specialist, Dr. Rahman, spoke. He wanted to remove the respirator.

As if she were invisible, Dr. Rahman stood beside her bed and used a monotone to explain how he would take the hose out. Doctors, nurses, Don and I gathered in close. We hunched and bent in, more anxious than a row of runners anticipating the crack of a start pistol, as he said to the audience at large,

"She will have to take a breath."

At that moment, Jennifer's life hung on her ability to understand language.

Dr. Rahman turned to her and said, "Be sure to take a breath." His stern face betrayed the fact that he was not sure she knew what he meant. The importance of this – like the importance of the first breath she breathed after exiting the womb – touched the rest of us, and we gasped collectively in response. Then Dr. Rahman turned and grabbed the hose with both hands, gripping it like a plumber snaking out a drain.

The eyes of those present followed his, Jennifer's most closely, as he concentrated down. We held our breath in sympathy, in anticipation, as Dr. Rahman yanked on the hose, using his arms and shoulders to pull it free. It came up and out of Jennifer, long and slimy like a big root, and it flailed in the air, as if it held the origins of life, itself. Jennifer arched up and pulled in a deep, thorough breath, filling her lungs.

Whispered Shame

My friend Jacqueline sat across the table from me in the Ruby Tuesday's diner of our local mall. Her pageboy hairdo fell just to her shoulders, around a face that was a conundrum. There was happiness there, a twinkling to the eye, an animated lift to the eyebrows and cheeks. I saw the touch of her artist's hand in the placement of her rouge and eyeshadow and lipstick. But there was heartache, too. The heartache rode on her eyelids, in the crinkles of her crow's feet, and in the very corners of her occasional smile.

It was as if these two emotions vied for supremacy, as if they had taken up some kind of wrestling match just under the top layer of her skin. I watched them throw themselves around under there. Flare in her nostrils. Shrink and swell in her irises. I watched Jacqueline take a bite of her steak – it was too rare, she sent it back – and I knew she was a reflection of me.

I was astonished at what my reflection showed me – all the ways life had settled into my face. The white hair that framed it was a shock, no matter how many times I saw it. And I thought that I pooched my lips forward more than I used to, like I was perpetually anticipating a kiss. I pulled my eyebrows down into a scowl, a learned habit, like Don's. I had face bags too, little puffs of fat that swung beneath my eyes and at the outermost edges of my chin. I sometimes hefted them up with my fingertips to find the young me hiding there. I recognized the young me. There she was, all hope and expectation. She was impossibly naïve.

I wondered how my face would have aged had life gone differently. Would it be less blotchy had I cried less? Would the lines wander different paths had I fewer angry moments, or fewer happy ones, for that matter? I felt my face scrunch into a wad as I pondered the possibilities. I felt the weight of my face – three pounds. If I could remove my face, I would lose three pounds. And that is all.

Jacqueline and I had a particularly futzy waiter that night. His contrived cheeriness and interruptions were annoying. All that prance to the table. All that coyness about our ages (Are we at least twenty-one?) when we ordered our beers. All that chirp about the dinner specials, the way he cocked his head and goaded Jacqueline when she didn't order a dessert. He was surprised when she returned her steak. "Rare" was apparently a matter of opinion.

What could that waiter possibly have known about rare? Jacqueline knew rare. And I knew it. We had lived rare.

"I'm not getting anywhere with community mental health and housing," I told Jacqueline, who had gone through the hurdles of moving her mentally and physically disabled daughter out of her home long before I even considered such a possibility. We had known each other for approximately five years, since working together at the newspaper. I bit down on a spicy piece of chicken. "Are you still happy with E's placement?"

I called her twenty-one-year-old daughter "E" because that's what Jacqueline called her. Like the young woman herself, her name, Elizabeth, had been truncated over time.

My daughter was luckier than E in one regard. Jennifer was still on her feet, be it ever so tenuously. E had been confined to a wheelchair since she was a toddler. And, while she'd gotten heavier – "fatter," according to Jacqueline – she'd also shrunk in a way. Her legs were contracted, as were her arms and hands. Pulled up as if her muscles were wound too tight. She folded them across herself, perpetually. She was stuck. A down-sized model of womanhood.

Jacqueline said yes, she was still relatively pleased. "Don't be mistaken, though. There have been problems. Would you believe I haven't seen her since before Christmas? I feel so guilty. It's so hard to move her. I can't lift her anymore. My knees just won't do it." Jacqueline diverted my gaze to one of her knees, protruding from under the tablecloth.

There was her knee, puffed and rounded like a Portabella mushroom.

"E weighs one-hundred-and-ten, now. She's fattened up since she went into the group home." Jacqueline smiled. A weight gain for E was a good thing. She could, after all, hardly take in food on her own.

I thought about how I brushed two sets of teeth every day, how I managed two menstrual cycles each month, dressed two bodies, tied two sets of shoes, combed two heads of hair, ran two baths, and I uttered a silent thank you that I didn't have to manage two meals three times a day, the way Jacqueline had all those years. At least Jennifer could feed herself.

I remembered watching E work to eat SpaghettiOs once. Jacqueline pried open E's contracted fingers and put a plastic, curved baby spoon inside them. E maneuvered the spoon in the air, swooped it in the general direction of her mouth, crashed it against her chest, and left slimy, orange Os on her over-sized bib.

"Once the group home staff got behind in dressing her for

school," Jacqueline said.

She paused and looked off, then continued to explain that it shouldn't have been a big deal. But the bus came and E wasn't ready. So they hurried her into her clothes. Snagged a shirt or a waistband – Jacqueline wasn't sure which – on her feeding tube and it came out of its anchor in her belly. She ended up in the emergency room, instead. There was a long wait. One thing led to another … a doctor's office … the hole closed up.

"Honestly, I was so upset. We thought she'd need emergency surgery," she said.

There, I saw it quite clearly now. Jacqueline's face was pursed. Heartache was taking this round.

"We got lucky this time," said Jacqueline. "The doctor was finally able to get the feeding tube back in."

I looked directly at her. Somehow, maybe because we were the same age, or maybe because we had a lot in common, or maybe because we were women, or maybe because we shared the bond of having raised disabled daughters, or maybe because we were both tired – too tired of the unimportant stuff anyway – we were able to talk deeply and honestly.

"Do you ever wish she would die?" I asked. Whispered it, really. Kept my voice way down low, so that no one else would hear. This was a wrong question. A terrible question. Maybe an inevitable question. I pushed the weight of it, the responsibility of it, off onto Jacqueline. She was pinned there, backed into the red naugahyde on her side of the booth.

Jacqueline met my gaze. She had pondered this before. Sat with it during one of those bottomless nights when a disabled child feels more like a ball and chain than a mother's flesh and bone. I could see this, somehow. The concept manifested not only in her forthcoming response, but in her facial expression. Jacqueline lowered her face so that her blonde bangs shadowed her eyes, but they were still directed at me. There was a subtle nod, a hint of I'm-tired-of-all-the-stress-too fellowship.

"What kind of mother wishes her child would die?" she pushed back at me.

Only a week passed before Jacqueline's and my whispered shame materialized, as if snatched from the air of our restaurant booth by an unseen demon, allowed to ferment, then swirled to unholy purpose. E suffered complications from her feeding tube mishap and, while hospitalized, went into a full cardiac and respiratory arrest that was initially believed to be a choking spell. Twenty minutes into her near death, the medical staff brought her back to an even more tenuous life. Dr. Rahman performed his duty over Elizabeth with the same bland resignation he had showed to Jennifer.

"He acts like, *why bother?*" Jacqueline confided to me on the phone during a call from work, and I understood. I remembered his attitude from Jennifer's near death – the way he quantified life, measured it by ability and not sanctity.

I told Jacqueline the one thing I believed to be responsible for Dr. Rahman's lack of compassion, for while working my old clerical job in the emergency room I learned one of the doctor's secrets. "He had a son who was brilliant, and he committed suicide when he was seventeen. Dr. Rahman's take on life has been tainted by that."

Jacqueline didn't seem particularly moved. Her thoughts were in the rut of responsibility. "I wish to God there was a way to take her home and not have my total life destroyed," she said.

Jacqueline's voice went down so that her co-workers would not hear. Her boss, expecting work as usual, was impervious to her situation, her fatigue, her worry. We disconnected, and later she sent me an email that said, "It has been touch-and-go for the last few days and there have been a series of very stressful and painful decisions for Bill and me.

"The good news is that while still not out of danger Elizabeth does seem to be a bit better today…. She has that 'ornery gleam' back in her eye and has reached for, and held on to, all of us who have been with her.

"And the good thing – seeing Elizabeth's innocent love has brought us all strength."

It had been years since I'd walked the halls of St. Joseph Mercy Hospital. The walls had changed since I worked there, since Jennifer was photographed as a nude infant, even since her brush with death. They were freshly painted, probably many times over. They wore new signs. They held up new floors and additions as well as a fair amount of decorative, life-affirming art. The hospital's administrators were trying to put an optimistic spin on illness and death. I located the elevator that used to take me to pediatrics, and I rode it past that old haunt on Four North, to the eighth floor, where Jacqueline marked time with E.

I entered E's room to find my friend standing over her daughter, fluffing blankets and stuffed animals around E's rigid, twisted body. Her head turned one way and her legs, drawn up, the other. Jacqueline pried E's contracted fingers away from their furious grip around the blue hose that came out of a hole in her neck. It wended its way from her windpipe and across her chest to the ventilator, which stood watch like a prison guard at her side.

"Breathe. Breathe," it seemed to bark at her with each blast of oxygen. Elizabeth fixed me with her eyes and traced my path to her mother, watched us embrace.

I spoke to E, greeted her in a voice that was probably too loud, even though I knew better. I had heard this done scores of times with Jennifer. People who thought words must be fired at full volume, lest they be lost altogether. People who thought sentences had to penetrate, like a barrage of bullets, to be effective.

"Hey, Elizabeth, how're you doing?" I leaned over her and

peered, as if she were in a display case. She stared.

I didn't expect an answer. Even if Elizabeth could talk, I knew the respirator would prevent it. I turned and ran the same question by Jacqueline, who was on edge, poised for action, her nerves anticipating that E's airway would clog, or the mechanical devices that monitored her would develop sudden glitches. Jacqueline pirouetted around Elizabeth's bed, speaking with a mother's soft voice, doing her best to coax a smile. She pressed the button on Elizabeth's musical stuffed duck. My question was less a question than an invitation into conversation.

We lowered ourselves into hospital chairs and began talking about every topic from work to men to art to bowel movements to death. We relaxed, finally, in the semi-darkness of Elizabeth's room, in the intimacy of this conversation, as if we were two women on a beach at sunset, with scarcely a care in the world. In the background the ventilator mimicked the sound and rhythm of waves. *Whoosh. Whoosh.* Sporadically, it offered beeps of caution, as if to remind us that even waves can harbor trouble.

Jacqueline, I knew, welcomed me in the form of diversion. I welcomed the connection too, understanding only too well how lonely and stressful a hospital vigil can be. Comfortable in our friendship, she quickly segued into talk laden with suppressed emotion, telling me she never grieved the loss of the hoped for, normal child that Elizabeth might have been. Elizabeth's symptoms, the result of a degenerative disorder called Rett Syndrome, came on gradually, like cataracts or graying hair, in a way that allowed Jacqueline to slowly, inevitably, change too.

There was a time when Elizabeth could walk and talk. Jacqueline produced a book she brought along to help E's nurses understand her condition, and she showed me pictures of beautiful little girls who would share Elizabeth's fate. I fingered my lips in concentration. I was thinking back to my first expectations of a normal, healthy child. Back to the way I put my own spin on the doctors' predictions – *slow to walk, slow to talk, mentally retarded.*

"I was in denial for five years," I told Jacqueline. "I just kept clinging to a hope that Jennifer was different, but essentially normal. I went through the mourning, though."

A nurse entered the room to tweak the dials on the machines and interrupted us.

Diverted, Jacqueline got up and cautioned the nurse to move Elizabeth as if she were made of glass. Her daughter's bones were so brittle that even the slightest amount of jarring could cause fractures. Jacqueline demonstrated the gentle lifting of a lifeless leg, and the nurse tempered her movements, while Elizabeth watched.

Jacqueline told the nurse that E could make some of her wants known by issuing blinks in response to questions.

"A long blink means *yes*," she said. Jacqueline leaned over E's face and asked for a demonstration. "Doesn't it, Elizabeth?" And the girl obliged by lowering her eyelids, slowly and fully. Her lashes were dark and long. Even from my spot across the room I could see them fold across her eyes, like those of an old-fashioned doll when cradled in a little girl's arms.

"It usually works. Not always, but usually," Jacqueline said, and she re-seated herself. Her demeanor was lightened by the nurse's attentiveness. Her response put Jacqueline at ease. I considered my friend and thought about how much I admired her, then brought her back into conversation with a question. "This all started because Elizabeth vomited and inhaled, didn't it?"

Jacqueline rolled her eyes toward the ceiling, then at me. Aspiration pneumonia. We didn't go into the details, but I knew we were both envisioning the retching, the panic that must have taken place in the backwash of vomit.

"Yes."

Jacqueline's *yes* carried the weight of implication – how this unfortunate pairing of body functions had changed their lives, probably forever.

"We have a long history with vomiting," I offered, thinking back over the countless events Jennifer had punctuated by throwing up, as children with Rubinstein-Taybi Syndrome and their lax digestive systems oftentimes do, and the way in which I had used my body to shield her from disgusted onlookers. "Jennifer vomits at the drop of a hat. Restaurants. Holiday gatherings. Company for dinner. Long trips in the car. On vacation. Waiting for a boat ride. At the dentist's office. Nothing is off limits. No scenario is too casual or too formal."

I offered these examples as I appropriated a mischievous facial expression and irony to my voice. I gave Jacqueline a sideways glance. I paused for effect and then told the story of an unhappy and particularly wicked nurse who couldn't accept this truth after Jennifer's knee surgery. How she believed it was my power of suggestion that made Jennifer vomit. How she ignored my warning and leaned over and poured liquid Tylenol down her throat with a snippy "Bottoms up!" I told Jaqueline how I wore Jennifer's vomit until shift change and the arrival of an understanding nurse, who loaned me a smock from the storage room. We were lost in vomit memories when Jacqueline noticed that an eavesdropping E was wearing her first smile in five weeks.

The Dream State

For years, Jennifer slept as if she were a contortionist – in an impossible seated position, curled over, her head between her legs, her face pushed against the mattress. Often she would pull the covers over her body, making herself a blanketed lump. This seemingly impossible position, doctors said, might keep her body breathing. She might have apnea.

For Jennifer, now in her twenties, and me there was no panorama of stars, nor even the neon signs of neighboring buildings. Our single window at the hospital where Dr. Stan had performed her leg surgery, a perfectly square, deep-set window, allowed us only to see into the adjacent room, which was filled with machines that had dials and tiny colored lights, not unlike the cockpit of an airplane. There were two chairs in this second room, one for the man who would keep watch on the machines and their readings, another for the guest who would keep him company all night – me, if I could slip away from Jennifer's slumbering form.

She was to sleep in a double bed, made up to look cozy like a bed from a country inn. There were sheets with matching pillowcases. A navy blue comforter with large pastel flowers stretched taut and precise across the top. Jennifer was to sleep in this bed after the attendants finished wiring up her head. Just a moment before, they had her seated in a chair, and they were spreading her hair into little even tufts with their fingers, as if they were hairstylists with a wish to create cornrows, and they were gluing electrodes, dozens of them, to her scalp.

Jennifer did not like this at all. She had an iron grip on poor Ethel, who like always she had brought along for company. Ethel's blond yarn hair, strangled by Jennifer's hand, stood in sympathetic disarray. And while Ethel's eyes would have bugged out of her plastic face if they could have, Jennifer's eyes moved manically, searching for something on a par with the cavalry – a unit of crusaders to save her from this fate.

Alas, all she had was me. I was worried, and I just wanted to get this sleep study over with. This suggested to her that I was on the side of the enemy. I even joined them in their battle cry, "You have to sit still, Jennifer."

We had brought a tiny red suitcase with a change of clothes, and I touted this trip as an overnight excursion – the kind she might have if she ever went camping, or if she were to spend the night with a friend. There will be interesting people, I told her. She would have a special breakfast.

Jennifer was a cynic. She knew all about hospitals, their familiar setting and scent. She remembered the ordeals of her leg and dental surgeries, not that far in the past. She understood the folks dressed in white, and she was sure I was giving off hot air. She whimpered a little, but not so much as to make a bona fide scene.

Once they had the electrodes in place, the attendants affixed thin wires to them and then, octopus-like, connected the wires to a machine that would monitor Jennifer's brainwaves while she slept.

I helped coax Jennifer into the bed, and meaning to comfort her, lay down beside her with an arm across her shoulder. I was in street clothes, and I felt somewhat as I imagined the suited-up Frankenstein monster might have, had he been allowed to lie beside his bride while she was jolted to life. I whispered in her ear, "Go to sleep now." I told her nothing bad was going to happen and encouraged her to relax.

She lay stiffly, Ethel jammed into her armpit, her head some kind of animated Sputnik sphere. Beyond the window, a young, burly, bearded man, a lumberjack type, waited for Jennifer to drift off. His was a practiced patience. She resisted, wanting to sit up, wanting to disentangle herself, wanting to thrash and then flee. The man was a paid voyeur. It was his job to stay awake all night to see if Jennifer stopped breathing. It is known that people with Rubinstein-Taybi sometimes have sleep apnea.

I pulled the comforter up over her to protect her privacy as much as possible. I closed my eyes and rested my head on a pillow, wanting sleep to be merciful and descend over both of us, but I could feel the man's stare on my skin. I felt my legs clamp, one against the other. I turned to obscure my breasts.

The more we tried to sleep, the more we itched, and the more we had to sneeze or cough. I was afraid one of us would fart and that it would reverberate over the man's monitor like a clap of thunder. I was afraid he would laugh at us. I worked to gently restrain Jennifer so that the electrodes did not pull loose. After a while, she began to doze and snore softly.

I bided my time beside her and soon, in a half sleep, she sat up. She put her stubby legs straight out before her, let her arms go limp at her sides, rolled her head forward and closed her eyes. It looked impossible. Her spine was rounded like a bridge. Her forehead almost touched her knees. Layers of stomach fat crowded one another like a pile-up of rubber rings.

I could not imagine how she could sleep like this, night

after night, but the doctors could. They had suggested to me that this was a position that facilitated her breathing. It was possible, they said, that her body knew it must sleep like this so that it wouldn't die. It was anybody's guess.

Jennifer had much less on her mind than I did, of course. Even if this bed were comfortable – even if there weren't a man watching – I didn't think I could sleep in it. My mind raced the race of sleep depriving exhaustion. I, too, wanted to toss and turn. To beat back fear. To hold Jennifer's uncertain future at bay.

Once she seemed fully asleep, I slipped from the bed cautiously so as not to awaken her. Mine were the movements of an accomplished gymnast. I inched my foot and leg out from under the covers, my hip slinking along. I pressed my toes to the floor, shifted my weight over them and allowed an arm and shoulder to follow. Once I had made a half escape, I tightened my abdominal muscles and circled my head and body around. With a controlled effort, I gained my balance and stood, attempting not to rustle my clothes. I held my breath because I was afraid the noise of breathing would awaken Jennifer. She sensed a change in the space around her. She shifted, moaned, looked vacantly up, drowsed again.

As quietly as I could, I tiptoed across the floor, snuck past the window and exited the room to join the man who was observing. Within moments I was watching, too. I took up the chair beside him and began my questions. "How is it going? What do the numbers on the dials mean? How can you stand to do this every night?" What monotony, I thought, hours and hours of watching someone sleep.

Beyond us, Jennifer hugged Ethel, fitfully. The monitor allowed us to hear her breaths and her night talk. Even in this state, she repeated her litany, "T is for… *Titanic.*" I waited for Jennifer to snort, to produce the animal sounds – the rooting of stridor, a windpipe obstruction once thought to be seizures

– that for years so frightened me, but she disappointed me. Instead, she roused and drowsed, roused and drowsed, and murmured like a toddler.

Finally, the man yawned and stretched and confided, though he stopped short of a medical diagnosis. "Jennifer does not stop breathing, but she is a very light sleeper. And she doesn't spend much time in REM, in the dream state."

The dream state. What an elusive state I now understood that to be. I remembered it from the good old days, when I could enter it at a moment's notice, with just a wink and a nod. I could cross the threshold to the land where anything was possible. I could walk on air. I could sing underwater. I could fly. I could change my gender, or grow fur, or fit through a keyhole in my dreams.

Definition Of Beautiful

Don and I sat in the bucket seats of our Pontiac, our arms cocked on the door handles, and we watched as Jennifer hobbled up the steps to the university cafeteria where she had at last gotten a job. She went across the gray loading dock and into the kitchen by herself on those winter days when the steps were free of ice. On the days when there was ice, one or the other of us took her by the arm and coaxed her along and up, as if she were a frail old lady who had forgotten her cane.

Like the other bottom-of-the-ladder employees, she had to enter beneath an overhead door that opened onto an often times fetid, greasy cement landing where deliveries were made, and from which empty boxes and garbage were dumped into trucks. There was one employee who hosed this landing down in a perpetual attempt at cleanliness, not so much for the employees' wellbeing as for that of the Department of Public Health officials who monitored such things. They poked their heads in sometimes to make sure everything was on the up-and-up.

During their breaks, many of the employees sat in ramshackle folding chairs, placed helter-skelter on this landing, and they smoked. The women gossiped with each other, mostly about the men in their lives, and every now and again their conversation was punctuated by a chorus of cackles that arose from them, as if this were a gathering of chickens instead.

The men, fewer in number, sat in a group of their own and talked about how they were going to move up in the world. Their voices were more muffled than the women's, more reserved, and they looked out across the parking lot, toward some manicured trees whose forms were as distant and vague as their and Jennifer's futures.

Jennifer passed these folks on her way to the time clock, which she never seemed to master. She found the time card with her name on it but was unable to line up the designated day with the punch of the hour. She slammed it down into the slot, haphazardly, searched for the box where the stamped card should hang, and put it away.

"How ya doin'?" she asked, broadly.

Her co-workers, who at first frightened me because they were unknown entities – strangers whom I would have no choice but to trust – adored her.

"Jen-ee-*furrr* ...," they shouted, welcoming her one at a time in raspy, smoke-tinged voices. Many had arrived before daylight to prepare breakfast for the students. Jennifer put in her appearance at a later hour, to make life easier on everyone and allow the cafeteria and its employees a pre-Jennifer jumpstart.

"Girlfriend! What happenin'?"

Some gave her high fives, others hugs, others playful jabs to the upper arm. The man who hosed down the loading dock flirted a little. All smiles, she smacked increasingly well-practiced high fives into their palms and picked up her pace, went into a gimp trot, entered the kitchen like a filly on a morning romp.

As she disappeared behind the more distant stainless steel

door Don leaned toward me and commented, "Just think. This is all she will ever have. This is the best she will ever do."

Don's demeanor was one of pride and absolute respect. I knew we were both thinking about her determination and how hard she had worked to get this far. Like me, he knew the stack of filthy silverware that awaited her was as priceless as a mound of ancient treasure.

A teacher in Jennifer's post-high school educational program, which she would attend until she was twenty-six, had gotten her this, her first job. In order to secure it, he had spent weeks negotiating with chiefs-of-staff, managers, semi-bosses, and job coaches. Then he came to our house and broached the subject one day, hinting around like he thought I might reject the idea.

"How would you feel ...," he began cautiously, sitting in our living room. He paused and watched for my reaction.

I waited, wondering what I was going to feel about ... *what*, exactly?

"... if Jennifer," again, a pause, "went to work at Oakland University?"

I could scarcely believe what he was saying. It was too good to be true. I leaned forward on the sofa cushion, feeling as if an angel had come to call. A job would further normalize Jennifer's life and keep her busy during the day. It would offer one more step toward her independence, a sign that Jennifer could fit into the world. "That would be wonderful!" I said. I wanted to embrace him, but didn't.

"We have a few students who work in the cafeteria, bussing tables, washing trays, sweeping. Maybe she could try," the teacher said. He was one of those wonderful, dedicated teachers who are always stumping on behalf of their pupils. "Just think, she'd be around people her own age. Other students." He went on to explain that she would be assigned a job coach who would teach her the tasks she would need to know, work alongside her for a few months until she mastered them, then gradually wean herself away until Jennifer was working independently.

It seemed too good to be true – Jennifer functioning in a productive way, in a public setting with her same-age peers. Jennifer's variation on *going to college*.

He added a cautionary ending. "We could try her at this but you'll have to be patient. Jobs don't always work out. Sometimes these students need to try more than one."

"These students" were the mentally and physically challenged who made up his caseload, most of whom Jennifer had gone to school with all her life. Young adults with guarded futures – with autism, mental retardation, birth injuries, exhausting motor tics, cerebral palsy. He offered to drive her for the first week and to find a college student who would then take over, a process that would last one semester. He wanted to move her away from her dependence on me. I wanted to loft into the air, and throw my arms around his neck. "Are you kidding?!"

He would later report to me that on Jennifer's first morning of employment, they became caught in rush hour traffic and she not only talked non-stop, she entertained herself by turning the radio off and on and riffling through his glove box. I remember that morning as beautiful and sunny, and I remember that I went about my own work with a sense of satisfaction and happiness. I remember thinking, *Welcome to my world!*

Rosetta, my favorite of Jennifer's co-workers, adorned in patchy oven gloves, set a large pan of chicken divan on a counter and yelled to Jennifer, "Wo-*maaan*, how you be doin' to-*da-a-ay*?" Rosetta was one of those tough but divine women who are all heart and practical life and open embrace. Her call to Jennifer rang the kitchen, went past the women who tossed salads, past the supervisor's office, and out to where the students loaded up their trays.

Jennifer loved that Rosetta could see her womanhood, she was empowered by that fact. She arched her back and pushed her bosom forward, flitted her hair with the fingers of one hand, mustered a blush.

At lunchtime, Rosetta helped Jennifer down the elevator to the women's powder room, where she perfumed her for fun and applied a generous dabbing of her purple lipstick to Jennifer's lips. Sometimes she brought a coordinating eyeshadow and nail polish. And sometimes her co-workers attempted to one-up her with a shocking pink or red. Always, always, Jennifer left work as if Aphrodite herself had anointed her.

"Wo-*maaan*, you be *beau-tee-ful* ...," Rosetta said.

Jennifer reminded me of this when I arrived to pick her up in the afternoon. With her peculiar little features, she had a vague resemblance to a female clown, a hint of one overlaying her face. I was hopelessly charmed and curled an arm around her shoulders, pulled her to me.

"Hey, Mom. Hey, Mom," she said. "I'm beautiful."

Speaking to me one day, Rosetta offered, "Wo-man," (there was just a hint of detachment, less playfulness, to the way she called me 'woman') "Jennifer love that silverware! Won't let nobody else near it." Rosetta shook her head in both amusement and admiration, wore a broad ivory smile across her lovely, dark skin. A wash of warmth and appreciation overtook me.

Jennifer stood nearby, at her wet-with-glop silverware station, a cafeteria hat that looked like a big white muffin perched cockeyed on her head, a white apron covered with stains embracing her belly. Broad as a canvas and coated with spaghetti sauce, melted cheese, salad dressings, soda drippings, and gravy, the apron had the appearance of a child's finger painting.

Jennifer thought no one could see those five pilfered bananas, curved lumps pooching through the apron's numerous pockets. She looked like the well-packed Annie Oakley might have looked before an especially vigorous gun exposition. Jennifer seemed oblivious to the truth that she could get fired for stealing food, despite the fact that she had been repeatedly warned.

Her supervisor, Joe, was a good-natured fellow, a man who liked and enjoyed her but who knew he must go through the ritual of reprimanding her when necessary. He delivered solemn little speeches to her when she had her hands in the goods, sometimes after I arrived to pick her up, thinking, I suppose, that I would support him. His facial expression was lost on Jennifer, but I noticed as he looked at me from over her head that he was barely repressing his delight at her moxie. I didn't tell him, but it was only recently that I turned her pants pockets inside out and showered my laundry room floor with a handful of multi-colored yogurt confetti.

She worked feverishly, matching forks with forks, spoons with spoons, and knives with knives, shoving them into dishwasher canisters then aligning those canisters in neat rows, like vegetable cans on a grocery shelf. She lifted a serving spoon and examined it closely, picked off a tidbit of lettuce, considered the spoon's size and shape, realized it didn't fit with the teaspoons and set it to one side, flicking the lettuce to the floor.

"*Everybody* be happy," Rosetta emphasized. "Everybody else hate that dirty silverware."

Serendipity had accompanied Jennifer's employment. Her co-workers had gladly abandoned the most filthy job to Jennifer's lack of savvy, which masqueraded as bona fide enthusiasm. Jennifer palmed and sorted this silverware with bare hands. When they became too wet she wiped them on her clothes, or flapped them in the air to dry them. She should have been wearing rubber gloves, but they were too large for her hands, too uncomfortable. She avoided them diligently.

Wondering if she also sometimes dined on the leftovers

from dirty trays – the half-chewed sandwiches, the broken cookies, the cola-tinted ice in the bottoms of glasses – I took her for a hepatitis vaccine, just to be on the safe side ... and, not really wanting to know the answers, I didn't ask any questions.

"I love my new job," Jennifer told friend and stranger, in every setting she entered. She was overcome with this love, certain that every banker, every pharmacist, every waitress, every pedestrian wanted to know – certain that everyone else shared her sentiment about their own jobs.

Sanctuary

Jennifer's room is a sanctuary for her, but it assaults my senses. Its colors and shapes clash, and there are odors that sometimes make me want to gag. The smells of shriveled French fries and dried-up garlic sticks, of molded apples or tangerines, of crushed peppermints or taffies or Tootsie Roll Pops – which she has squirreled away in her dresser drawers or within her pillowcase or under bracelets in little jewelry boxes – overlay those of sweated-through socks and tennis shoes, and urine-stained underwear, heaved recklessly into a corner. Sometimes the candies lose their shape as they age, and melt down over old pennies or nickels that she has also hidden away, so that the coins get sticky and give off an air of metal mixed with flavoring.

There is the scent of her skin and oily hair on her bedding, and of dust too. The dust is particularly pungent in the area of her television, where the machine puts out enough heat to change the way the dust smells, to give it a cooked-dust aroma.

When Jennifer is home, the television runs all day, whether or not she is watching it. She turns it on first thing in the morning, with her first step out of the bed, before she has even gone to the bathroom, and turns it off just before she douses the light at night. She frequently fidgets with the volume. As the day progresses, she cranks it up loud, so that the television can be heard over her tape player, which she plays at full volume, to drown out the television.

Back and forth the noisy competition goes until the ceiling vibrates in our dining room, and either Don or I run upstairs to tell her to please turn it all down.

Outside in the hallway as I approached her room one day I heard the voices of Fred Rogers or Kermit the Frog or Lawrence Welk or Barbara Walters challenging Wynonna Judd as she belted out, over and over, "Tell me why-yi-yi-yi." Jennifer never let Wynonna get past this line. She stopped the tape in the same place, then rewound and replayed and stopped it, again and again and again, so that Wynonna began to sound as if she had the hiccups.

I mumbled to myself as I found Jennifer's door, "Tell me why, indeed."

Above and beyond the volume of the tape player and the television, I could hear Jennifer singing. She had the tune to *Tell Me Why* down pat, but she was making up her own words, screeching happily into the air, "Why-I-No-Na. Why, why-Nona. Bri loves Sar-ah." If she had to, she rushed the words to keep up with the music's tempo.

The Brian of Jennifer's song was the handsome actor Brian D'Arcy James in *Titanic*, the Broadway musical, and Sarah was Sarah Brightman, of Andrew Lloyd Weber former wife/pop opera fame. In Jennifer's mind, Brian and Sarah were lovers. They had kissed aboard the *Titanic*, which, to Jennifer's way of thinking, always floats.

They had done what lovers do, and Jennifer was delighted. At age twenty-five, she wanted somebody to kiss. When she was not singing, I heard Jennifer talking out loud about love. She talked to Brian D'Arcy James as if she were a four-year-old and he was an invisible friend standing next to her.

"There's a Valentine dance in Feberry. Martin'll be there," she said. "Valentine dance. Valentine dance. Valentine dance."

Whenever her crush Martin, a mentally disabled man, box stepped Jennifer around the gymnasium floor, he held her close to his body and stroked her face and hair with his palm. Jennifer shone when this happened, as if she were being polished. Martin was almost two feet taller than Jennifer, and she gripped his waist and rolled her face upward to find his half-closed eyes. Jennifer looked like a girl straining to see in the curtained windows of a skyscraper. Together their bodies moved in an awkward clutch, oblivious to the rhythms of piped-in music.

"Martin'll luv me," I heard Jennifer predict. "And we'll be there. Martin and I'll marriage in seventy-five years." Jennifer sighed wistfully over this magic number. The dream of love was enough to keep her going. Seventy-five years until companionship. Seventy-five years until glory.

I pressed down on the handle that opened Jennifer's door and stepped into her green and blue room. She was, as usual, sitting on her bed's comforter with her collectibles gathered around her, and she was sorting them, which she did endlessly. There was a pile devoted to cassettes and audiotapes, and another pile devoted to shells. She had three souvenir jewelry boxes lined up near her feet, and they were opened to reveal necklaces and rings she had grabbed out of the treasure box at the dentist's office. The understanding Dr. Spangler has always indulged Jennifer's greed for plastic jewelry. Turned a blind eye when she pocketed more than her share.

Next to Jennifer, on a small table, was her stash of unopened water bottles and juice boxes, and framed photographs from her high school "graduation" several years before.

Mainstreamed into general education classes but unable to

genuinely compete academically, Jennifer earned a "Certificate of Completion" after finishing twelfth grade at age twenty-one. When she limped across the stage with her normal peers at commencement, she turned herself into a star. A pudgy diva in cap and gown, Jennifer went center stage and blew kisses to a standing ovation.

That night, in a twist of serendipity that must have been masterminded by angels, the community sponsored an all-night graduation party with a *Titanic* theme. In one bedside, silver-framed photograph, her favorite, Jennifer stands with three friends, waving from a balcony converted to a ship's deck.

Behind Jennifer on her bed, lined up like soldiers along the headboard, was her stuffed animal collection – Flounder from *The Little Mermaid,* Ethel the Cabbage Patch doll, lions and bears given by carnival gamers who had hearts bigger than their lust for Jennifer's money, a host of Beanie Babies.

Above her, around the walls on bookshelves or old-fashioned hooks was a series of mementos that honored her obsession – *Titanic* posters and a painted wooden plaque with dates and statistics, a bright silver ornament that captured the ship in its heyday, a cast-iron *Titanic* bank with iceberg lever, picture books and videos that documented the history of the *Titanic.* Overseeing all this, at an angle to Jennifer's window, hung a black and white caricature of her that was drawn at the graduation party. Curiously, the artist had captured Jennifer's face as if it were that of a normal woman. It depicted her aura of accomplishment and delight, but omitted the distortions of her mental retardation syndrome.

In the drawing, Jennifer looked mischievous and full of life. Her eyes glinted out from behind glasses placed evenly on her face. She had a big caricature head with flyaway hair, too. It was drawn above a miniature body clothed in T-shirt and slacks. Her left hand held a diploma. The right was angled upward from the elbow, a finger pointing over her shoulder toward a tiny image of her high school friend, Julie. "That's a picture of Julie," the artist wrote to appease her. I could only assume that Jennifer chanted about Julie while he did his work. "*Joo*-lee. *Joo*-lee. *Joo*-lee."

I was intimately familiar with the things in Jennifer's bedroom because I was intimately familiar with Jennifer. I was the one who cleaned it, and cleaned her. I was the one who noticed when something changed which, aside from her health, was rare. Change in the life of a mentally disabled adult is predictably minimal. Sometimes Jennifer managed to form a coherent sentence and eke out a new idea. "What's going on down the street?" for example. And occasionally a peer placed a phone call to her, invited her to do something fun. Most often, though, change came in the form of a fishy taint in the air, a betrayal of the onset of illness.

Once every couple of days or so I went into Jennifer's room when she was off at her job, and I sorted through her belongings, not to be meddlesome but to help keep her physical life in order. I pitched out the food she'd scavenged and vacuumed the carpeting. I organized the clothes in her closet. I emptied the pillowcase and washed it along with the sheets and blanket. I read through the paper scraps, mostly tattered love letters she managed to scrawl to Martin. I folded them neatly, and put them in her top drawer.

It came as a big surprise to me one day when I entered Jennifer's room to find something genuinely new – little red dots spotting the window and far wall, just beneath her *Titanic* ornament. From the doorway, it looked as if someone had taken a Magic Marker and pressed out a series of specks. The speck on the window glowed an especially beautiful and iridescent red, the sun highlighting it as it shined its way into the room. The red specks against the light-blue walls had a somewhat brownish cast, like birthmarks.

Curious, I made my way across the carpeting for a closer

look. I leaned in, my face inches from the wall, and peered through the lower half of my bifocals to see that Jennifer had Scotch-taped ladybugs where they landed. They were posed in all directions, caught in the moments of their deaths, with their shells folded closed, consumed by little serrated cellophane squares, a retarded variation on bugs trapped in amber.

We were having an infestation of ladybugs. The weather had taken on a fall chill, and the bugs had come into the house seeking warmth. I had seen them clustered at the corners of the den ceiling, grouped inside the shade of our dining room light fixture, and wandering in twos and threes around my ironing board and kitchen sink.

Ladybugs are my favorite bug and I have been known to spend too much time simply watching them. I delight in the simple beauty of their high-shine, nail-polish coats, and enjoy remembering, as I consider them, the childhood rhyme, *Ladybug, ladybug, fly away home. Your house is on fire. And your children all gone.*

I had no idea why Jennifer had Scotch-taped the ladybugs to her wall but I was moved by the sight. Moved like I would have been if I were pondering a Van Gogh or a Rembrandt.

When she arrived home from work, I walked with her to her bedroom and asked, "Hey, Jen, what made you tape these bugs to the wall?" I feigned the demeanor of a mystified, inquisitive child and waited to hear what she would say. I knew any explanation would come with difficulty and have no genuine meaning, and I really didn't expect much. But still, I was curious. Curious about why she did it. Curious about what kind of explanation she would attempt.

Jennifer shrugged her shoulders and slurred to me, "I 'unno." She looked at me with her Rubinstein-Taybi face. Her green eyes sloped downward. Her nose, like a thick crooked finger, pointed at me. Her grin was a toothy, lazy rubber band oval. Jennifer laughed the laugh of a tease, and turned to her television. I walked away none the wiser.

I left the ladybugs where she taped them until it was time to repaint her room. I got up close to the wall for a second time and imagined Jennifer as she must have looked when she performed the deed. I imagined her thus passing the time on a boring Sunday, her plump little hands with their square-tipped fingers and jointless thumbs grappling with the tape dispenser. I saw her working hard, concentrating, tugging off pieces suitable in size for ladybugs. She waddled the length of her bedroom wall, from right to left, lurching on one long leg, and one short one, happily engrossed in the task of sticking this bug first, and that bug next. I pictured the bugs too surprised to flee or fight, going calmly and with resignation to their deaths. As I considered them, unbidden came the question – What, if anything, does death mean to Jennifer? I formed my left thumb and forefinger into little pincers and peeled the ladybugs delicately away from the wall, knowing that I would have to settle for theory over answer. Guesswork has always been the biggest part of raising Jennifer.

It may be that she taped the bugs to her wall and window to allay her boredom, it may also be that she was attempting to preserve beauty. Another guess came from the part of me most vulnerable to fear. Did Jennifer wish to send a message? Perhaps she could express with ladybugs and tape what she couldn't express with words – I want to stay here. Forever.

Lovebird

"DeAR MARTIN,

"YOURe CUTe AS Me AND TARA DANce WITH LOVe OF YOU AND Me TO YOU AND eVeN DAWN MARTIN I WILL WeAR A JeWeLY HeART INSIDe OF Me AND I LOVe YOU SO MUCH ANYWAY I DO MISS YOU AND BRIAN D'Arcy JAMeS IS A SINGeR AND I DID CARe ABOUT THe WeD-DING DAY FOR US IN LOVe WITH YOU AND I THINK ABOUT. WHeRe We MeT AT THe WATeR-FORD OAKS AND I DID BeFORe YOU KNOW IT I GUeSS SO SWeeT BOYFRIeND I eVeR SeeN IN MY LIFe. SOMeHOW I DO NOW. TO BeLIeVe IN Me AND YOU GO TO THe GReAT LAKeS CROSS-ING MALL GOT eVeRY THING We NeeD TO DO SOMeTHING LIKe THAT WAY YOU DO BeFORe I DO NOW YOU WANT TO Be MY HUSBAND AND I GOING TO Be A WIFe AND ON A DATe FOR YOU AND MORe YOU AND Me I AM GOING TO Be A BRIDe AND YOU WeAR A TUXeDO AND

AT THe MALL HAS THAT AND YOU WeAR A
BOWTIe AND SO I CAN DO SOMeTHING eLSe
AND YOU DO UNDeRSTAND Me AND TOMOR-
ROW IT WILL YOU WRITe Me BACK TO Me.
LOVe JeNNY LAURIe WALKeR APRIL 15, 2003."

I went to the mailbox just after lunch to retrieve the handful of bills and advertisements the mailman had left. I dipped
in with my right hand, forgetting that Jennifer's love letter to
Martin was there, where I saw her put it, gently and hopefully,
the day before. The letter came into my fingers along with the
mail, and I noticed as I turned it over that it was slightly bent,
the address running in a stretch away from me, as if it genuinely
wanted to transport Jennifer's message to the destination she
had written – DIXeHIGHWAY NeW HeRIZen NOW. There was
no stamp. There was no street address or city or zip code. There
was no return address. There was, however, an eagerness in the
way she had written *NOW*. The word, in all capitals like every
other word except those containing the letter "e," was huge and
firmly pressed in place. It raced to the edge of the envelope,
where its mission was punctuated with a distinct black period.

My heart sank because I knew she would never receive a
reply. Martin was never going to write her back. Martin was
never going to marry her.

The letter would never go any farther than, where? I
wondered what I should do with it. Should I throw it into
our kitchen trash? I thought not. Such an act seemed almost
sacrilegious to me. Jennifer had sat before the television and
worked for over an hour composing it, methodically putting
down each letter, as if laying paving bricks in a doll-sized patio.
She asked me only, "How do you spell tuxedo?" And I told her,
my heart embracing her passion. Should I store it in a box with
baby pictures, holiday cards, and kid drawings? No, it was not
meant for me. Should I take it down to the postal box on the
corner? I could drop it in there the way I used to drop her let-

ters to Santa Claus.

It occurred to me that the letter, if mailed, might actually make it to the sheltered workshop, New Horizons, where Martin worked. A savvy mail carrier could figure out where to take it. The spelling was not off by much.

The county dances where Jennifer and Martin danced were wild affairs, where shuffles and stomps passed as the fox trot or waltz, and flails as the tango. As far as I knew, Jennifer had actually danced with Martin at three of approximately a half-dozen dances. There were a couple where he was a no-show. At those, Jennifer hovered by the door, dejected but dedicated, waiting for Martin to make his appearance the way a dog awaits its master. I always stayed at the dances, a silent observer who couldn't bear to leave her daughter under the supervision of adults we didn't know. I loved watching the two of them be-bop around the room. It broke my heart to watch her on those nights when Martin didn't come, ignoring the other young men she could have partnered up with, preferring instead to while away her time in her one-sided romance.

I was reasonably confident that Jennifer had proposed marriage to Martin the third time she saw him. He had said to me when I pulled her out of the bear hug in which she'd clamped him, "We're just friends." And he refused to give her his phone number. You don't give your phone number out to strangers, Martin had informed Jennifer and me, as he walked in the sunset toward his father's car.

Jennifer didn't care. She gushed as he drifted out of sight, her cheeks all aglow, "I'm engaged." She said those words regularly after that, and once she even asked me, "Are you going to come to my wedding?"

It was true, as she had written, that Martin was cute. He was a tall and nice-looking man in his early twenties. Preppie in style, he had well-groomed hair and was given to wearing sweaters, khaki pants, and brown dress shoes. In her letter, Jennifer likened his cuteness to her own, as well as that of Tara, a friend of hers from school. I was not sure why she did this, except she liked to say as she had for years, *"T is for Tara, tickle, trombone, and ... T-T-T-Titanic!"* In Jennifer's mind there was some sort of obscure but joyous link among all these things.

The also mentioned Dawn was a teacher's aide, expected to chaperone at a class dinner dance that was planned to usher the twenty-six-year-old Jennifer and two other young adults, finally, out of Michigan's public education system. I could see when I read the letter that Jennifer was blurring the dances in her mind, plotting them to ensure that Martin would appear. I knew she would be disappointed again. The school dance bore no affiliation to the ones where Martin box stepped her to elation.

In a similar fashion, Jennifer blurred her hearts, which she understood to be the seat of love. She knew of the heart that beat inside her chest, and she knew of the jeweled *Heart of the Ocean*, cast overboard by the love-struck *Titanic* heroine, Rose. Brian D'Arcy James had an affiliation with the *Titanic* as well. He was a singer who had captured Jennifer's obsession in Broadway song.

I knew I could help Jennifer's letter find its destination, that I could fix the address and place a stamp in the envelope's upper right-hand corner, but I didn't do this. I didn't want to invite the people who worked at New Horizons into Jennifer's fantasies. I didn't want them to micro-manage her love for Martin. Instead, I brought the letter, envelope and all, into my office and placed it in a drawer, where it would be safe.

By October of that same year, some six months after she wrote her letter, Jennifer had thrown over her affection for the love-shy Martin, and, seemingly without so much as a second thought, had given her heart to the more enthusiastic David, a friend of hers from SCAMP, who was as trapped in his body as a mummy in its sarcophagus.

David called her almost every day. The telephone rang and I jumped up to answer it because I was, even though moderately arthritic, swifter on my feet than she was. I heard his man's voice gather its wind and attempt to phrase her name when I picked up the phone. "Is Jshenny home?"

He worked his tongue over the consonants as if he were scraping melted cheese from the roof of his mouth. Jennifer, nine months shy of twenty-seven, was almost always home, and I fetched her while he waited.

"Jennifer! David's on the phone!" I called as I took to the stairs, hoping my voice would penetrate her bedroom door, beyond which Celine Dion crooned the love theme from *Titanic*, while Jennifer worked the CD over the same phrase again and again, *my heart will go ah, ah; and ah, ah; and ah, ah; and ah, ah; and on and on....* I detected a dip in the volume but not too much. She cranked the door handle hard, opened it and flapped her arms, wing-like, then step-thumped her way past me and down the staircase – which took considerable time – through the living room and into the kitchen.

I watched her step-thump with her head held high. She was pudgier than ever now, an enlivened dwarf on parade. Wearing enough necklaces to stock a display case, including her replica blue heart honoring the *Heart of the Ocean* thrown to sea in the *Titanic* movie, she whipped them to a shoulder with a wave of her neck, picked up the receiver, smiled broadly, and placed it to her ear.

David was most patient, awaiting her presence on the phone, I was sure with a great deal of anticipation. I backed out of the kitchen, allowing Jennifer a woman's privacy for her conversation, but it didn't matter. Even if I went back upstairs or out on the lawn I could hear her shouting her high-pitched affection. "David, I love you! I love you, David!"

There was a pause, just long enough for David to say, "I love you!" back. I knew the duration and the speed of the three-stroke tempo these words commanded. Their conversation was always the same, limited to love and the memories of first meeting, limited by the constraints of their willing but impossible bodies and lust.

"David, I met you at SCAMP," Jennifer screeched. In her room she stowed away pictures that showed the two of them on the beach, embracing at water's edge, frothing with desire as if they were Burt Lancaster and Deborah Kerr filming *From SCAMP to Eternity*.

I wondered what David was thinking on his end. What kind of woman he might otherwise romance if his legs could bear his weight, his lips produce a kiss. Though physically disabled in nearly every way, he was much brighter than Jennifer, and he knew that he had met her at SCAMP. I pictured him receiving her comment as if he were truly astonished, for Jennifer's sake. He seemed infinitely patient, but perhaps patience came second nature to him, a necessity, bound as he was to a life without mobility.

Strapped for hours at a time in his wheelchair or in his hospital bed, David had little to occupy him besides his thoughts. I had my suspicions about his cunning – how he must have prodded the attendant at his group home to dial the phone for him, how he probably urged her to hold the receiver to his ear but to not listen in, how he must have plotted to find time and place with Jennifer.

The day came when he placed a personal call to me. I heard him emit a tongue-manipulating, "Woul' shou bring Jshenny over to shee me?"

I was seized not only by his effort but the longing in his voice, and I committed to honor his request. I heard myself say, "Sure, David, of course I will." Some part of me wanted Jennifer and David to share in the euphoria of romantic love. I remembered how love had energized my life when it came to Don and me, and philosophically, I believed that they were equally entitled. But some part of me was terrified, too. Would I have to chaperone their marriage, dole out her birth control? Would I have to comfort her with words she couldn't understand if love, or David, died?

While few have given birth, it is known that women with Rubinstein-Taybi have a high likelihood of passing the syndrome onto their children – giving birth to miniatures of themselves who have beak noses, sloping eyes, jointless thumbs, and stymied IQs. And as if that weren't frightening enough, I know that Jennifer's peculiar little body could never carry a child, to say nothing of her inability to raise one.

All her life I fought for her right to lead an independent, full, and rich life – to strive for her potential, the way the rest of us do. I took on school systems so that she could be placed in classes with higher functioning students who might challenge and encourage her. I pressured the medical establishment, and I fought for her job when it was threatened due to a change in management. Now here we were at the pinnacle of that effort and I had to ask myself if she, if I, dared make another move.

Sometimes it would have been better if I were the proverbial fly on the wall – a slightly less obtrusive and annoying presence. But as it was, on this particular day when I took Jennifer to see David, I was antsy, seated on a cream-colored, cushy sofa, surrounded by way too many throw pillows, and amazed at Jennifer's behavior just across the room. I was struggling to control that amazement, keeping my voice in check, trying not to lurch and jump every time she made a move. These were the behaviors I'd displayed all her life – my maternal efforts at reining her in when she promised to get carried away.

Jennifer, her enthusiasm propelling her forward, was seated on the very front edge of an oversized footstool, and David was in his wheelchair before her. His attendant in this county-run group home, named Danetta, had gone to another room to fetch the carnations David had bought my daughter for Sweetest Day, although Jennifer was unaware that such a holiday even existed. The toothless Danetta, grinning and chatting affectionately, was delighted by the idea of their love and, in cahoots with David, had planned a grand presentation for the flowers.

While she was out of the room, Jennifer clasped her hands together and shoved them between her knees, tilting her head coyly to one side and batting her eyelashes, as if she were a purring actress in a Rudolph Valentino film.

I could scarcely believe what I was seeing and hearing. She appeared to have absorbed every hokey gesture from every Big Screen romance she'd ever watched and made them her own. Jennifer preened, she fawned, she swooned. Her hands went before her breasts now, her voice suddenly Bette Davis-deep, airy and sensual, something more than a whisper.

"I love you, David. I'll be the best, brightest babe you ever knew." She shook her head gently for effect while David looked on, his face reflecting infatuation and amusement.

Danetta, before going for the flowers, had retrieved David from a nap for this, Jennifer's first visit with him outside of SCAMP. They had not seen each other in months.

Because Danetta didn't attach the foot rests to David's chair, his legs hung awkwardly, suspended like those of an abandoned marionette when the strings are too tight. His right foot began to shake up and down uncontrollably, like Thumper's in the movie *Bambi*.

I knew David was excited – just as besotted as Thumper – what I didn't want to know was *how much*? I engaged my rational mind. His foot thrummed the air because some obscure nerve lost in that tangled body misfired. He was not, please, have mercy, sending Jennifer sexual messages that were beyond me.

Jennifer was so completely unabashed about her intentions. She reached forward and clamped David's twisted fingers in her hands. I could not tell from my position if she was squeezing, as she was sometimes prone to do.

"Don't hurt David," I yelled, finally overriding my restraint and going to sit beside her.

David's head went way back so that he looked at the ceiling. This response was part delight, part cerebral palsy asserting itself. He urged his face back down.

"Don't worry, I will shay shomeshin if she doesh." He directed his voice to me, but his eyes were on Jennifer.

At this, she released his fingers. I noticed the blood drain back into their tips. She grabbed the armrests of his wheelchair. With mind-boggling speed and agility – as if she had both practiced this maneuver and honed her strength on a rowing machine – she swept his chair and him between her legs. He was there in an instant, his knees brushing her inner thighs.

David was thrilled. And I was mortified, at Jennifer's audacity and at my unspoken concerns. I noticed the taped corner of David's paper diaper peeking over his belt. The sight was both reassuring and heartbreaking to me, but Jennifer paid no attention. Her face was more alive than I had ever seen it. "David, I love you," she gushed.

As if on cue, the carnations presented themselves. David took them from Danetta, gave them over with a strained reach, and Jennifer accepted them, but she was much more interested in a hug and kiss.

I watched, entranced and curious, as she rose and went to embrace his shoulders. Stretched to full length, she stood at the same height as David when he was seated. The woman inside her knew what she wanted. She claimed herself, planted a kiss on his cheek, pressed herself against his chest, lingered there, and David attempted to wrap his all but useless arms around her.

Danetta and I uttered sweet, stereophonic *Aws* – as if our

voices were being piped in from two sides of the room.

When Jennifer's hug became a little too eager, I peeled her off David and insisted that she sit back down, and attempted to conjure up small talk. As a distraction, I helped entertain their fantasy as David and Jennifer began planning their first date. She wanted to have dinner at the Red Lobster, while he preferred a movie. My mind whirled. Yes, I would drive her to meet him if an attendant could get him to a rendezvous.

David, showing the stunning depth of not only his affection for, but his understanding of Jennifer, said he'd been working on a picture of the *Titanic* for her but had not been able to render it perfectly because he couldn't draw well. It would come eventually, he said. Jennifer went wild at this news, hooting and clapping at the prospect that a portrait of her obsession would be given to her by the man of her dreams.

Suddenly she wanted to see David's bedroom. She asked boldly, "Can I see your room?" Jennifer arose once again, pivoted David's chair, and began nudging him down the hallway as Danetta and I followed, like two anxious cocker spaniels.

David's room turned out to be a sparse affair, dominated by his bed and a hoist on one side, and an empty bed that awaited a new client on the other. Things were in a bit of a clutter. I could see how he must have pored through his open drawers recently, dropped his belongings, been forced to leave them on the floor. His sheets were in disarray. On his brown dresser there was a stereo system, his prized possession, and beside that at somewhat of a distance, a silver urn that Danetta informed me contained the remains of his mother.

I was at once struck by what seemed a macabre addition to an already uncomfortable environment, filled with compassion for David, and reminded of my own mortality. His mother had been dead just over a year. I envisioned the woman she must have been, long in the limbs and dark-haired like David, her face impossibly forlorn. I noticed the way my own spirit wanted to step in as surrogate. I felt her giving me a nudge from the other side.

Danetta stood behind David and mouthed the unspeakable to me with her gums and lips. Her mouth was a tiny, dark hole. "His father doesn't want anything to do with him." She worried her hand in front of her face.

Unable to see her (and me hoping that my expression didn't betray the truth), David broke the silence now monopolizing the room, speaking of his mother's death without betraying a single emotion, while Jennifer, at his side, made a mental connection and announced, "Your mother is in heaven."

"I hope sho," David said.

In what seemed like short order, we lost track of David. One day I simply noticed that the phone had stopped ringing. There was a subtle change to the overall tenor of our noisy household.

Certain they must miss one another, I thought about David and Jennifer's love. I felt optimism pull at me, a quixotic notion that I could rectify this, that I could nudge along something akin to happiness for them if I tried. On a scrap of paper I wrote *Find David,* as if he were a misplaced screwdriver. I left the reminder on the kitchen countertop, where for weeks I shuffled it around lunch fixings or dinner dishes, waiting for the day when I would have time to commence a search.

We learned of his February move to a new group home when I phoned Danetta to schedule a visit between Jennifer and David. He had been swallowed up by the community mental health system, and moved without notice.

"David doesn't live here anymore," Danetta said bluntly into the receiver. Her voice pitched up and tantalized with possibility. "He's somewhere closer to you, supposedly."

I sighed. David must be waiting out there in the world, full of hope. I thought that he was close in the same way that a moon on an elliptical path sometimes moves in on its planet, even as the forces of nature push it away.

I am ashamed to admit that I ate the red heart box of chocolates Jennifer had bought David for Valentine's Day. They would be stale by now, early June, was how I rationalized my behavior. I said to myself, "We can buy more," but I wasn't fooling anyone. Store shelves were stocked with Fourth of July fireworks and beach toys. There wasn't a red heart box for miles.

David would have been thrilled with that heart box, too. He, the quintessential romantic who said to me during a visit last Christmastime, as he handed over a bottle of perfume to Jennifer, "She told me over the phone she wantsh to kish me." He caught my gaze with his own, blushed, and followed up with a copper ring for her finger – a hand-me-down, dime store band inherited from his cousin. "Can I ashk her to marry me now, or do you want me to wait?"

David's question hovered in the air and then dropped into the hole I reserve for questions with impossible answers. I felt it hit bottom. "Maybe you should wait," I said.

From his wheelchair, after I located him through our community mental health channels a full two years into their hit-and-miss relationship, David finally orchestrated the most perfect date with Jennifer that he could. It was the kind of date Cinderella and Prince Charming might have had, if the clock had not struck midnight just when things were going well for them. David called on a weeknight and pronounced with an empowerment that I couldn't help but admire, "I've made plansh for ush."

I listened.

"I bought ush ticketsh to the prom. They were thirty dollarsh."

I thought about the magnitude of this expense in his government-funded life, and I heard myself agree to bring Jennifer to his special education school on the appointed night.

He wanted to know what color dress she would wear, and I said pink, knowing all the while that Jennifer would show up in her good white slacks and a mauve blouse. It is impossible to fit her body into a dress, and I have long since given up trying, but how could I explain this? Why would I want to go into all the details at that very moment?

"Jennifer will be excited," I told him.

The evening was, as David would soon observe, perfect for a prom. The weather was clear and tepid. The sun burned a marvelous tangerine figure into the sky, evoking just the right dose of romance as it did so.

We arrived at the prom ahead of David and were greeted by a bevy of enthusiastic PTA mothers bent on making this a memory-worthy night for their children. Most of those in attendance were students of the school, young men and women in their early to mid-twenties, with all manner of complicated mental and physical disabilities. Jennifer seemed to be the only outsider, but not for long. She was, as I like to call it, "fully gussied" for this affair. Accenting her silk blouse, she had on four bracelets, nine of her favorite beaded necklaces, in all colors, everything from wooden to glass to shiny metal, and four plastic rings lifted from the dentist's treasure box.

She quickly ingratiated herself as she announced, "I'm waiting for my husband. He's my best true love I ever met. I'll be his lovely bride."

Her comment was met with a series of smiles and hums, the mothers looking at me with understanding.

Jennifer squealed when she saw David's van finally pull up. He exited it with help from an aid, dressed in his best clothes, twisted to dating perfection in his wheelchair, with a pink corsage pressed into his hands.

"Mom, it's so romantic," Jennifer gushed. She was feigning

Valentino kitten again. "Here comes my best, true love."

I slipped the corsage, which David said he had ordered only this afternoon, onto Jennifer's wrist for him and she surprised me when she said, "You can leave, Mom," as she gripped the wheelchair's handles and pushed David toward the action.

I was a confusion of emotions – proud of her and delighted to be sharing in her delight, afraid to leave her in a crowd of strangers, touched by her desire for adult independence even as I was aware that she was still mostly a child. We compromised when I drifted off to the far, distant end of the cafeteria, way beyond the dance floor – beyond even the disc jockey and the dining tables to a bench in no man's land, where I set up watch like an owl on a barn rafter.

The evening's festivities began with a song, Prince's *Let's Go Crazy* – which struck me as a somewhat ironic choice, given the scenario. I couldn't help but wonder about the DJ's sense of humor. From my spot as spy, I noticed that Jennifer and David were totally involved already. They were oblivious to those around them – the stumpish girls who swam in their oversized evening gowns, the spastic break dancers, the ecstatic young Down Syndrome man who was on the receiving end of a bump and grind.

Jennifer and David held hands. They hugged and kissed. They paused and gazed into one another's eyes. They did the arm polka, Jennifer moving David's left arm up and down as if she were dancing with an old-fashioned water pump.

After an hour, the mothers served up a chicken and rice dinner, but Jennifer and David scarcely seemed to eat. I knew from experience that excitement had claimed victory over Jennifer's otherwise insatiable appetite, but I was not sure about David, who was something more than a paraplegic, something less than a quadriplegic. I ambled over, and not wanting to embarrass him, asked him in a whisper if he needed help with his food, and he told me that he did because he didn't want to spill on his good clothes. It would be different back at the group home, he acknowledged. There, he could spill all the food necessary to get some into his mouth. But on a date, especially this date ... well, things were different.

I seated myself next to him and began to fork rice into his mouth. Jennifer did not take this move well at all. "I want to do it," she said, summoning a pushiness that was new to both of us. "Let me do it!"

Surprised, I handed the fork over and watched while she delicately speared a piece of chicken and moved it to David's lips. As he rolled his head back and opened his mouth to receive it, I was amazed by the way he completely submitted to her.

She pushed the food at him tenderly, more tenderly than a mother bird might feed her tiniest, most favorite fledgling. She had every muscle and nerve in her body focused on his satisfaction, and I could not help but realize that a woman I had never known now sat before me.

The Longest Walk

During the decades since Dr. O'Neill stood at the side of my hospital bed and told me, for all practical purposes, that Jennifer would not be retarded, I never asked him about his decision to sugarcoat the truth. I was afraid to. Afraid that I would offend or hurt, or worse, anger him. I was afraid that in tone or words I would take out my frustration about the injustice of Jennifer's condition on the very person who least deserved it – the one person who, unfailingly, had believed in and tried to help both her and me.

Instead, I cast him the benefit of the doubt. I chose to believe he meant well, that he didn't want to devastate me with the equivalent of an emotional flogging so soon after her birth. His was an act of sensitivity, of mercy, I told myself. And I decided that he wasn't really sure about her, anyway. Who can settle on a lifelong truth after only one visit? Would another doctor have done differently, or better?

I also considered that he was afraid I might fall apart. Perhaps influenced by the opinions of his peers or by the tenets of his education, perhaps based on experiences with other mothers

– what other kinds of mothers could he have dealt with? – he might very well have assumed that I would go numb in the bed and refuse to get up.

Maybe a hard truth is just not the kind of thing a doctor delivers in one-fell swoop. Maybe it's better given in increments, measured and weighed carefully, portioned out for adequate digestion like unpleasant medicine. He couldn't have known a well-intentioned nurse would show up the next morning with a book about retardation and cast doubt over what he'd said the night before. He couldn't have foreseen everything.

There were plenty of times in the years that followed Jennifer's birth when I thought to myself that Dr. O'Neill was right not to tell me she would be retarded when she was born. It was better that he allowed me time to hope and come to terms. Time to fall in love.

I never stopped to think about the fact that he must have had feelings, that he must have brought his own emotions to Jennifer's situation too. I didn't think about how tired he might have been researching in the library late into the night after a long day in his office, or about the fact that he'd probably never seen a human being with RTS before and was trying to figure things out, or what it must have been like to anticipate my reaction. I didn't think about any dread he might have felt before he entered my hospital room, or the joy he must have known would be inevitable if we could just keep Jennifer alive.

"It's the longest walk of your life when you have to tell a parent his or her child is dead or handicapped," he said to me one day when I was visiting with him in his office, something I did more and more over the years. I can't know how much Dr. O'Neill said to other people or how much time he spent in their presence. But my years with him had been kind.

I don't remember what prompted his remark, but when he spoke, I imagined for the first time what the long walk to me must have been like for him – the deliberate stride I'd come to recognize, his arms swinging, his blue eyes aimed toward his destination, his mind formulating the sentences he would have to say, and the order in which he would say them, the calling up of his courage. I wondered how many times he'd made such a walk in nearly thirty years of practice. I pictured him in a pitch-black corridor, moving toward me like a reluctant beam of light.

One day though, unexpectedly, I finally realized why he didn't say what he didn't say all those years ago. It was a truth I'd never considered. The revelation enveloped me, as warm and welcome as sunshine. I was beside him in the hallway of his busy new clinic, the one he'd finally brought to fruition after years of planning and hard work. He wasn't dressed in the white lab coat he'd worn for so long. Instead, he had on a blue pediatric shirt with primary-colored bears all over it. Nearing seventy, he was more stooped than he used to be, more fragile, and his hair and beard were a shock white, not the premature gray-white of our first meeting. Some of the bears lay across his belly, and some crawled up his back. A few adorned the short sleeves on his arms.

He took the health insurance forms I handed him – they were considerable – and he set them on a little table that folded away from a wall. He rested the edge of his belly there too, and he looked down to begin filling in the information required to maintain Jennifer's health insurance. She was an adult now, and the insurance company, through Don's employer, wanted a reason why they should continue to insure her beyond their cut-off age of twenty-six. The forms sought information about everything, in particular whether or not she was permanently and totally disabled, and to what degree.

I watched as Dr. O'Neill wrote a lot of mumbo-jumbo in classic, doctor-scratch cursive. I saw all kinds of commentary, but not an actual reference to her retardation, the most important issue. There were vague references, innuendoes and implications, but not the concrete language that would help us.

I was long past political correctness when it came to Jennifer and terminology. I despise the word *retard* when hurled as an epithet, and I challenge people if they use it in my presence. But *mentally retarded* is acceptable to me in the context of diagnosis or services. I don't find it offensive, it's simply true. And it's much more manageable than the cumbersome *mentally challenged* or *developmentally delayed* that is used now. A rose is a rose, after all …

A vital part of Jennifer's future hung in the balance of this transaction.

"You need to tell them she's retarded," I said to him. "Please don't mince words. You'll have to be direct or she could lose her medical insurance." I was almost frantic, adamant, caught up in the potential of such a significant loss. Jennifer's health was expensive, and without medical insurance her care would greatly diminish. It was a terrifying thought.

Dr. O'Neill looked up and directly into my face. He flicked his pen, like a cigar, between his first and second fingers and spoke. "It hurts me to use that word."

I was stopped by what he said. His admission tugged at me and I choked back the affection I had come to feel for him. In the silence that ensued, my mind raced back to the first hours of Jennifer's life. I may have given birth to her, but he cupped her essence in his hands, like an offering, when he came to talk to me that night.

Jennifer's Weight In Paper

As a lover of trees, I sometimes wonder how many have been sacrificed over the years to keep up with the paperwork needed to move Jennifer's life along. Her various academic planning meetings have resulted in a file that is almost as high as the cabinet that holds it. Her chart at Dr. O'Neill's office weighs nearly as much as a dictionary ... and that is the chart of just one doctor. Now that she is an adult there are forms needed for implementing her independence – agency forms, employment forms, housing forms, financial forms, insurance forms, legal documents.

As provided by Michigan law – so much of her life is governed by well-intentioned laws – Jennifer attended public school until she was twenty-six years old. She was identified as a special education student but was allowed to participate in general education classrooms whenever possible. The last four years of her education were spent in what is called "post high school," where the focus was on living and employment skills and not on math and reading. The closer she came to the end of this education, the more her teachers encouraged Don and me to place her in an independent living situation. Everyone knew the term "independent" didn't really mean "independence." At a bare minimum, Jennifer will always need one responsible adult roommate and someone to oversee her financial and personal needs. It meant independence from her parents and a sense of ownership of her own life.

The teachers reiterated the importance of this fairly frequently, noting that it is normal for young people to leave home for college dormitories or apartments. "It's healthy and appropriate for everyone concerned," they said. "It's what happens in the normal course of events."

Soon we had been funneled to the county agency that oversees these kinds of placements, and Jennifer had practiced her independence at what is called a "respite" home – a group home where eight or so "clients" stayed for up to two weeks at a time, giving their parents a bit of freedom for vacations and so on. Jennifer adjusted to these weekends well and the next step was undertaken – finding her a permanent place to live.

I had visited several group homes when I was a reporter, writing features about some that had received community awards, and in one case interviewing a senior citizen who, following his move into a group home from a mental hospital, had been reunited with his brother after decades of institutionalization. The visits helped dispel some of the mystery and anxiety for me, as the people living in these homes, as well as their staff, were generally happy and involved in life.

Don had not had the benefit of such exposure and instead had only the long-distant, unpleasant memory of his aide job in a mental institution for comparison. Because of this memory, his sense of responsibility, and his love for Jennifer, he was inclined against placement. I knew he would gladly keep her home, where she was safe and well-cared for, for the duration of our lives.

Another thought niggled at me during those years – I

wanted to place Jennifer while Don and I were still young and healthy enough to monitor what happened to her, to have some say in her destiny. I didn't want to have her placed in a group home during an emergency or a death – thus having to deal with two traumas instead of one. An emergency placement wouldn't necessarily mean a *good* placement, and I didn't want the responsibility for all this change to fall to Holly.

Whenever I raised this topic in conversation, Don would pivot sideways and look into his lap to avoid eye contact. And I'd bear down on him with my eyes.

"I know it has to be done at some point," he'd finally say, his expression clearly betraying his sadness over this truth. "I know it has to be done." Even simple change has always been difficult for Don – he would protest whenever I moved the furniture around, or wanted to repaint a room. Sameness and safety are synonymous to him. The prospect of this change seemed almost insurmountable.

While I might have appeared somewhat callous to him – although he never said that – my heart identified with his and I felt torn between my maternal instincts, a sense of wifely duty, my own insecurities, and my need for action in light of an inevitable future.

Ultimately, as we waxed and waned in our decision, it took three years, until Jennifer was nearly thirty, to find a home that we considered decent enough for her.

We had high standards, insisting on safety first, then cleanliness and same gender roommates to minimize the possibility of sexual activity. What we wanted, but could scarcely dare to hope for, was a home like ours. We visited two apartments in which there would not be staffing at night – we couldn't even begin to entertain such a scenario for Jennifer – before we were finally introduced to Claudia, a woman who, experienced in this kind of caregiving, would make our transition almost effortless.

"God has given me a calling," she said when we were introduced to her. She made eye contact and stood confidently, with her back erect, and I felt my fear begin to melt a degree or two.

Once we had seen her place, a three-bedroom modular home with bright white walls, a cozy fireplace, and cheery decorations, I felt confident that an arrangement could be made and I approached Don to elicit his views – and to urge a little, if I had to. He was seated in his tiny upstairs office, paying bills.

"What do you think?" I said to him, leaning against the doorframe. My nerves felt like taut rubber bands as I awaited his answer. He had maintained his physique for all these years – even his hairdo had not changed – but he looked fragile, his cheeks hanging as if they were half-filled sacks. He had the lights off and evening darkness was descending around us. He didn't answer.

"Do you feel like you're abandoning her?" I asked. My own sentiments tended in this direction – it was the only sentiment I could imagine either one of us realistically feeling. We had learned at Holly's wedding a few years prior that it's hard enough to hand a daughter over to a groom who's been coming around for a while – let alone hand one over to a complete stranger.

"It feels a little like abandonment. Yes." He coughed up this truth, shook his head moderately, looked at his lap. He licked a flap and worked his fingers over a bill envelope. Sealed a heavy payment inside.

I already had Jennifer's move mapped out in my head. The way we'd box up her environment (and her trust) – her *Titanic* treasures and Ethel and her stuffed animals and her CD player and her television and her knickknacks and her clothes – and transfer them to our van under her watchful eye, then unpack and place them strategically in her new room, so the strange would feel like the familiar, so she'd feel at home right away.

Jennifer, I thought, will be a mother hen of activity that

day. She'll manically pocket her trinkets, a sort of knee-jerk protection. She'll raid the kitchen one last time, snatching as many crackers and Popsicles and cheese slices as she thinks she'll be able to get away with. She'll tromp up and down the stairs with the kind of skepticism she manifested whenever suitcases were produced and there was a change in our family pattern – be it hospital stay or vacation or trip to the beach. She'll flap her hands. She'll chew her lower lip. And she'll thread an anxious whine into her voice because, while part of her won't understand what's happening, part of her will.

Of course, Don and I will have explained the move to Jennifer several times by this time. "It's like an apartment," we will have insisted, but we will affirm this again. And again. For her sake as well as our own. "You're going to have a roommate, the same way Holly did. It will be fun!"

My mind wandered back to the campy college chaos of her sister's first apartment. The bead curtains separating bedrooms. The ramen noodles littering the floor. The ins-and-outs of a seemingly endless stream of friends. I thought of Holly's occasional phone calls for comfort and money.

I was so grateful that Holly had set a precedent. The fact that her sister moved out first, in the normal course of events, made Jennifer's tearing away just a little easier. Because of Holly's example, she would have a visual image to cling to, one with a positive spin, and not some nebulous sense that she was being abandoned. Or so I hoped.

Our first interview with Claudia, during our initial visit to her home, spiked tension in me more than any interview I could remember from my years as a reporter. My insides squirmed as Don and I ushered Jennifer through the front door of her impeccable home. Claudia stood in the distance, in the shadows. When my eyes adjusted to the change in light I noticed that she was somewhat older than me, her hands were clasped, and her short brownish hair was woven perfectly atop her head, as if she wore a beautiful, inverted basket. I scooted Jennifer around Claudia's living room, around the end tables, the rocking chair, the knickknacks, and the houseplants as if I were pushing a grocery cart in an obstacle course, in search of a user-friendly seat for her.

As we maneuvered, I was struck by this thought – those white walls will never stay clean. Their semi-gloss shine will soon be streaked by Jennifer's fingerprints.

Over the years, I had watched her smudged fingerprints spread the length of our walls, ascending from just a foot or two off the floorboards to as high as my belly, as she grew. If I looked close enough I could see the accrued, textured remnants of old tomato sauce meals and sticky desserts – byproducts of her perpetual parade from kitchen to bedroom and back to kitchen.

John, Jennifer's mental health caseworker from the county, who for two years had been searching for a place where Jennifer could live, stood off to the side. His face was lit up with satisfaction as if he were a streetlamp topped by a shiny new fixture. He had, he believed, found a place that would please us – safe, clean, loving, reliable, licensed, and available.

We took a brief tour of Claudia's home and then dropped down into chairs around the dining table. Don and John sat quietly, Jennifer guzzled some Kool-Aid, and Claudia responded, unfazed, while I put her through an auditory gauntlet. The mother of a daughter, herself, she seemed to understand my core fears. "What makes you want to take in handicapped adults? Do you bring men home? How old are you? How's your health? What will you do in an emergency? Do you have a criminal record?"

Claudia was nothing if not a good sport. She answered honestly and politely, as unflappable as a goose without feathers.

With Claudia, the only thing missing was a shared history.

We didn't have the bond of parents who've spent months planning their children's wedding and who've just watched them walk down the aisle. We didn't have a cherished childhood friendship that kept us close. We didn't know one another's secrets. We didn't even have the advantage of relay runners. True, Don and I would hand Jennifer over to her like those runners hand over their batons, but we could only hope that the teamwork would gel later.

Now it was Claudia's turn to see our place and we sat at our dining room table, our first dinner together behind us. We all made it through the put-on-our-best-selves phase. We relaxed some. Our conversation became more casual, less forced. We melted into the ambiance of the dining room – the lingering aroma of the grill, the hum of the nearby refrigerator, the cream glow of the ceiling lamp, Claudia and Jennifer and me listening to the gentle padding of Don's and Christian's feet as they shuffled off to their beds over our heads.

"Would you like to see some pictures of Jennifer when she was little?" I asked.

This was a method-to-my-madness brainstorm on my part, a way to sweep her into our lives, to connect more deeply. She would see that we'd had our struggles, but she would see happiness too. She would see that Jennifer had been well cared for and deeply loved. I wanted Claudia to know these things. I wanted, I suppose, for Claudia to think well of me.

Over the previous few months I'd added to my conflicted feelings about this move a sense that I had not or might not measure up as a mother. I'd been caught in the complex emotional flux of a mother who felt like she was giving her child away. With the aid of our photographs I saw my adult life pass before my eyes and wondered how a woman can feel like she's drowning when she's actually reaching the top of a mountain. I pulled in a breath that shuddered my body, rested my chin atop one fist, placed that elbow next to my plate, and offered commentary as I handed pictures over to Claudia, Jennifer's life fanning by. My head bobbed up and down on my fist as I talked.

"Isn't she adorable? See, she didn't used to be so chubby. She's the cutest punkin in that pumpkin patch, isn't she? That's Jennifer with Ethel after her leg surgery. In this one she has a Special Olympics medal. She's climbed in the kitchen cupboard in that one. See how much hair she had when she was born! That's one of her and Cookie Monster."

Claudia looked at the photographs patiently and passed them to Jennifer who chimed in with her own fond memories. When she put them down, Jennifer carelessly smeared her fingerprints across our past.

A few weeks later, committing myself to one last, efficient purging of Jennifer's bedroom, I found in her drawers a bowl of stale cashews, four wrapped slices of petrified cheese, a handful of party crackers, several dollars' worth of swiped pennies, marbles, shells, rocks from the yard, rainbow-colored rings from the dentist's office, miniature Smurfs and Cabbage Patch dolls, five broken CD versions of *My Heart Will Go On*, which Jennifer had attempted to fix with tape, one Popsicle stick, licked clean, and a jewelry box full of sunflower seeds.

It was moving day, a Saturday, and while Jennifer watched television in our bedroom where she'd been banished for the duration of this process, I solicited Don's help with her desk, a heavy, white monster we had purchased only weeks before as part of a new bedroom set for Jennifer. He had his back to me and I could see his muscles twitch through his T-shirt as he worked to pull three stubborn drawers out of the desk, which we were determined to move to Claudia's. Don was committed to lightening its load so the two of us could carry it downstairs and out to the van. The drawers relented slowly and stubbornly, symbolically I thought, only to reveal at last a hodgepodge of gone-missing junk backed up deep behind them, as if wedged in the farthest reaches of a series of caves.

Shaking his head in amazement and disgust, Don reached in and pulled forth a crinkled, *Titanic*-emblazoned T-shirt, another CD, some fake bead necklaces, loose change, a glossy country western magazine, folded photographs of David, and tiny squares of paper that Jennifer had cut with scissors during her idle time.

"It's amazing that all that stuff fit back in there," I observed, wondering how she managed to shut the drawers. Don turned to hand me a faded white plastic box, its window top snugged on tight.

I recognized the six-inch box as having belonged to his mother. I took it and peered in, just beyond a foggy strip of tape that Jennifer had fastened haphazardly atop it. The box contained one spotless ladybug that had been spared from the wall taping. Moved by the metaphoric nature of this creature, I hurried and hid it in my own dresser drawer for safekeeping.

On the evening of Jennifer's move, Don was well into a nap in front of our bedroom TV. Claudia would be arriving to claim her at about 8:30 PM. The reporter-cum-memoirist in me had been taking notes all day, a task I found myself involved in as I flitted my nervous energy from one room to another. I felt moderately guilty about what I was doing, like I was both a mother and an opportunist. Nevertheless, I knew that someday I would want to remember the details for writing purposes, so on my scratchpad I noted Don's position along with the aside that our old SCAMP favorite, *Sunshine On My Shoulders,* was being played on *The Lawrence Welk Show.* Then I peeked into Jennifer's bedroom to see that she was on her bed, bouncing to the music. She spied me and wondered out loud when Claudia would arrive.

"Soon," I told her, tugging her door behind me. I stepped downstairs and walked around the main floor of our house, tidying up loose ends, placing last-minute movables near the front door, distracting myself with busy work. Feeling a sense of impending loss, I was determined to save my tears for a private time, and when they started to surface I forced them away with a blink and a good throat clearing. Outside, night fell from a cloudy sky.

When Claudia finally marched herself up to our front door I fetched Jennifer, who accompanied me like a child being led to Santa Claus, and she and I greeted Claudia with broad grins, Jennifer's natural, mine forced.

"Let me go get Don to say goodbye," I said as Claudia stepped inside. I bolted back up the stairs and nudged him awake. "Jennifer is getting ready to go."

He mumbled an "all right" as he stretched, and we ventured to the living room together, trembling the air with our scarcely suppressed emotions.

Jennifer was eager. As she scampered toward the door, she spoke to Christian, who was crouched on the living room floor sketching in front of the television, as if this were just an ordinary evening. As if his sister was simply on her way to buy shoes. Without looking up from his drawing, he replied with a soft "bye".

Christian was sixteen now and small for his age. He was obviously gay, and recently diagnosed with the autism spectrum disorder Asperger's Syndrome. He had become an increasingly distant planet that circled the sun who was Jennifer. The bullies at school had discovered him, and, consumed by his own challenges, he was mostly unable to relate to Jennifer's. While she talked a nonsensical streak about the *Titanic*, Christian spent his free time funneling his thoughts into the fantasy characters he liked to draw over and over and over – a witch, a princess, and a hero.

A decade later, while riding beside me in the car, he would confide the thoughts he kept to himself the day Jennifer moved out – that he was relieved to at last have quiet in the house, and that amid our family chaos, the world of fantasy felt most like home to him.

Jennifer hugged Don and me by turns and we proclaimed our love to her, and she to us, like echoes. *I love you. I love you. I love you.* Then I grasped the doorknob to steady myself and turned to see my husband quietly hunching his way into the kitchen. He was en route to the comfort of ice cream, something to keep his mind and heart distracted.

It goes without saying that for Don and me this was one of the hardest things we have ever had to do, second only to burying Matthew. This change was infinitely harder than bringing Jennifer and her mysteries home from the hospital after her birth, anticipating the ways she would affect our lives.

Claudia beamed upon this scene and then took Jennifer's hand to lead her onto our enclosed front porch. She followed agreeably like a little child, and I couldn't help but wonder what was going on in her thoughts. Did she simply think she was off for some overnight fun comparable to that she experienced at SCAMP? Did she fathom that she was moving away permanently? Was she happy about this, or resentful in a way she couldn't share? She didn't seem afraid.

As Claudia and Jennifer stepped away, stepped onto their toes from off the porch and out onto the sidewalk that led into the world, as lightly as Dorothy and the Scarecrow ventured forth on the yellow brick road, I found myself compelled by one last maternal dictum.

"You behave yourself," I quipped to Jennifer, as if this admonishment could set her straight for the remainder of her life.

Hearing my voice, Jennifer let loose of Claudia's hand and turned to face me. She was wearing her mischievous version of the Rubinstein-Taybi face, the one that is all merriment and promise. Her eyes were crinkled and full of life, her smile was broad, her eyebrows lifted, her head tilted in a happy but exasperated, *Mother, puh-lease*. Without speaking, Jennifer raised her right hand, its jointless thumb cocked just so, and she saluted me.

A Moment Of Astonishment Hung In The Air

By the time Jennifer was an adult, we, her family members, had begun to hold her up as an ideal. The realization that her experience of life might be something to envy rather than pity had crept over us like warmth from an ascending sun. We had come to recognize the wholesomeness with which she saw life, to admire the way she unabashedly embraced it. Another person's color, nationality, religion, sexuality, age, gender, or station in life, was of no consequence to her. There was no place on earth that didn't have its merits, there was no task that wasn't worth trying, there was no person who couldn't be friended, and there was no fraction of time that didn't contain some measure of joy.

"Everyone should be like Jennifer," we would take turns saying.

Therefore, when a letter arrived at our house suggesting that scientists were on the verge of a treatment for Rubinstein-Taybi Syndrome we found ourselves amazed but indifferent. I was on my way in from an errand when my hand plucked the letter from the mailbox. My thumb tore through the envelope's seal. Unsuspecting of course, I opened the letter and read it with bland curiosity. It had been sent by a mother representing the RTS parent group that had grown out of the Cincinnati conference with Dr. Rubinstein, and as I read it I was jolted into the moment. It said:

> *RTS is caused by a mutation in the gene responsible for a very important protein called the Creb binding protein, or CBP. Individuals with RTS have less CBP than they need.*
>
> *Earlier this summer, two highly reputed research teams published their results of projects that proved CBP has a critical role in memory and learning. Both teams were successful in restoring and ameliorating some of the cognitive and physiological deficits in RTS mouse models by administering drugs that are currently being tested for us on Huntington's disease and cancer.*
>
> *Both teams suggest that the mental retardation associated with RTS may in part be a result of the body's lifelong need for functioning CBP. This scientific discovery has the potential to change the lives of people.*

There are no words to explain what it is like to learn – long after falling in love with your disabled child and seeing her through thick and thin into a reasonably stable adulthood – that maybe, someday, she might not have to be retarded anymore. An image of Don and me, innocent as two cherubs, watching the scientifically enhanced Charlie and his dead counterpart, the mouse Algernon, flitted out of dormancy into my consciousness. Could the makings of fiction possibly become our new reality?

I called Holly, desperation to share this news having overtaken me as I awaited Don's arrival home from work. I whispered her name into the phone as if I were blowing out a candle, *H-h-h-holly* …

She responded *yes*, the way she said it clearly indicating that she sensed I was about to say something unexpected … something important.

I could feel, in my flesh, the intensity with which she listened. We were as connected by the telephone line as we once were by the umbilical cord. "… I just got a letter that says scientists have found the cause of Rubinstein-Taybi Syndrome and there is a potential *treatment!*"

A moment of astonishment hung in the air.

"What! Are you kidding?" she said. "Read me the letter!"

I read it, the words sizzling as they left my tongue.

When I finished, our reactions scattered like mercury dropped on the floor. We had no time to gather or discuss them. Don walked in, interrupting our conversation. I kept the receiver to my ear and passed him the letter, my few words conveying the gist of it in an exaggerated whisper, "They think there's a treatment for Rubinstein-Taybi Syndrome!"

I watched his eyes go down to scan it, watched them surface, two divers coming up for air. He handed it back to me with his typical shrug and went to put water on for tea. I followed him with my eyes, anticipating a reaction, anticipating that he, like me, would be mind-boggled. When none came, I disconnected from Holly, stepped away from him and, cradling the letter in my palms as I would an open book, took it into my office, slipped it back into its envelope, and then into a drawer for later consideration.

It took a full day for the information to sink in. Holly called back the following afternoon. "Mom?" She sounded hesitant. "What's it like? What does it feel like, after all this time, to finally know?"

I didn't know how to answer. Of the many words – of the *implications* – contained in that letter, it was the word *protein* that came to the forefront of my thinking. I pictured a genome – that is, I pictured what my imagination believed to be a genome – and in the center of all its DNA and genetic code I saw a six-ounce hamburger on a bun. I wondered – has Jennifer had a lifelong need for a functioning hamburger? It's silly, I know, but I couldn't, in my wildest imaginings, fathom where it must have been that a protein had gone wrong. Nor could I fathom its god-like powers.

I said, "I don't know" to Holly. I raised my eyebrows and threw a hand in the air, as if she were standing in front of me and could see the gesture.

The letter, of course, had been sent to other parents of children with Rubinstein-Taybi Syndrome, and I wondered how they responded when they received the news, standing in their kitchens, wearing their shock like Halloween masks.

In addition to explaining the important information, the letter asked for donations so that the researchers could complete their projects. It showed an emotion-tugging photo of the letter-writer's son, his face a version of Jennifer's – a version of every person with RTS who has ever lived. The mother's hope reached off the page as if it had fingers, and touched me.

We sent the requested donation, and then occasionally talked in hypotheticals – is it better to be innocent or learned? How might Jennifer feel to wake up a new person and to recognize all that had been amiss for so long? Could we bear the thought of releasing the child we love to a different version of herself?

It was good after thirty years to know the cause of RTS. But any real chance for a cure seemed remote, unpredictable and unnecessary. An invasion into the love we felt for Jennifer. Without ever mentioning the letter to her or seeking her opinion, Don and I abandoned it to the collecting of dust.

Jennifer's Best Day

Jennifer begged me, sometimes overtly, sometimes slyly, to take her to see Celine Dion in concert. She had learned while listening to the radio at Claudia's house that Dion was headed our way in September, shortly after my birthday. Jennifer had taken to suggesting that one occasion deserved the other. "… and then it will be your birthday, and then we'll go see Celine Dion," she would say, mischief and expectation alive in her Rubinstein-Taybi face.

I knew that seeing Celine Dion in person would be the most exquisite experience for Jennifer, whom I felt, after a lifetime of challenges, deserved to have this wish fulfilled. I had tried for years to get her to explain her fascination with the *Titanic* and *My Heart Will Go On,* but she was unable to. She couldn't articulate her thoughts and emotions, or the associations the song provided. She could only play the song over and over again, as if she couldn't get enough of it, as if it quenched a thirst far beyond the reach of water.

I bought three tickets, and a friend and I took Jennifer to the concert on a lovely, warm evening. Don, a homebody, chose to stay home, and if I live to be one thousand years old I will never understand how he could miss what we both knew would be Jennifer's greatest delight.

Jennifer bounced in a stadium seat between my friend and me, her eyes absorbing Dion, long and slender, as she cavorted onstage in the distance. For over an hour she had sung her way through some of the songs Jennifer knew – she noted each one she owned, sang along with a few – but I knew she was waiting for *My Heart Will Go On*. She was electrified with anticipation. Occasionally she leaned into my ear and said, "She is going to surprise me." Jennifer was certain Dion was going to sing especially for her.

But as song after song began and ended she worried that her favorite was going to be omitted. She scoured the program, and found the coveted title crowded amidst dozens of others positioned in an artistic font at the back. She gestured at it with a forefinger to remind me of its importance. At one point, swelling with joy, she leaned over and hugged my neck, kissed me on the cheek, and clearly said, "This is the happiest day of my life." The suspense was almost more than I could bear.

Finally, Dion sang what appeared to be her last song, not *My Heart Will Go On* but a Motown tune meant to leave goodwill with her Detroit audience. Her face lit up a screen in front of us, while Jennifer's, now crestfallen, cascaded down her chest and into her lap.

I leaned in to Jennifer to say – hoping with a hope like Peter Pan's when the children clapped Tinker Bell to life – "I think if we call loud enough she will sing the *Titanic* song." I demonstrated a robust yell, feeling confident that Dion had saved her signature song for the encore. The concept of an encore was one I couldn't explain to Jennifer through the noise of the thundering crowd, although I tried. She followed my yell with an urgent hoot.

And then it happened. The auditorium, its lights darkened, shrank around my daughter like an iris around a pupil. I became part of an eye that focused on her as the words and notes of *My Heart Will Go On* arose from their source to alight on her like a mist of perfume. Jennifer gave off an unmistakable glow colored in the pinks and yellows of a ripe peach. Her face went still. She swayed her arms and hands above her head and turned her eyes heavenward, held this pose like a saint seeing a vision. Jennifer had gone to a place where the rest of us could not go. She was deep inside the Rubinstein-Taybi body that once so puzzled and unnerved me. Jennifer had gone to dwell in her happiness. I will admit, had she invited me to accompany her, I would have followed.

THE END

Acknowledgments

There are scores of people who deserve to be acknowledged and thanked for their contributions to Jennifer's life, as well as that of our family – doctors, teachers, friends, relatives, and kind strangers.

I wish to particularly thank the doctors and staff of Shriners Hospital in Erie, Pennsylvania and their orthopedic surgeon Dr. Karl Frankovitch, Dr. James O'Neill, Dr. Craig Spangler, D.D.S., the late Dr. Stanko Stanisavljevic, Fran Eldis, Ph.D., and the late Barbara Greenstone.

I wish to thank the SCAMP program, its staff, and Jennifer's peers.

I wish to extend my deepest gratitude to Vermont College of Fine Arts and its faculty, especially Erin McGraw, Robin Hemley, Bret Lott, Ellen Lesser, Laurie Alberts, Christopher Noel, Phyllis Barber, Sue William Silverman, Natasha Saje, and Larry Sutin.

In addition, I want to extend my appreciation to the VCFA Director, MFA in Writing program, Louise Crowley, as well as my friends and peers who read portions or all of my manuscript and encouraged me – Margo LaGattuta, Susan Martin, Joan Cohen, Kathie Giorgio, Kathryn Kay, Deb Zaslow, Andrew Massey, Esther Fine, and Maggie Kast.

About The Author Carolyn H. Walker

Carolyn Walker, a former journalist and columnist, now publishes as a memoirist, essayist, and poet. She is also a long-time creative writing instructor for Writers Digest University online, as well as other schools.

She began writing as a young child, and after working twenty-five years as a reporter, publishing in a variety of Michigan newspapers and magazines, she ventured off to graduate school and earned her MFA in Writing degree from Vermont College of Fine Arts in 2004. She specializes in Creative Nonfiction.

Her award-winning writing has appeared in *The Southern Review, Crazyhorse, Hunger Mountain, The Writer's Chronicle, Gravity Pulls You In: Parenting Children on the Autism Spectrum, HOUR Detroit, The Detroit News*, and many other publications. Her essay "Christian Become a Blur" was nominated for a Pushcart Prize and reprinted in the 50th anniversary edition of *Crazyhorse*. In 2013, she was made a Kresge Fellow in the

Literary Arts by the Kresge Foundation.

She is currently working on two new books – *Questions Counted Like Stars*, a memoir about the challenging childhood of her gay, mildly autistic son, and *You Live by Luck*, the story of growing up with her zany mother and steadfast father, a World War II veteran.

A lifelong Michigan resident and the married mother of three grown children, she is a gay rights and disability advocate.

She has an interest in travel, Michigan history, and the stories of everyday people, quietly going about their lives. She finds that she encounters them everywhere.

Made in the USA
Columbia, SC
15 April 2017